THE GENDER PENALTY

TURNING OBSTACLES INTO OPPORTUNITIES FOR WOMEN AT WORK

ANNELI BLUNDELL

Dedication

—

To Sienna.

*This book is dedicated to my confident, cheeky,
creative and courageous teenage stepdaughter Sienna.
May you never need the words on these pages.
But if you do, let the stories of these wonderful women
bring you insight and understanding, and inspire you
to make the world a better place.*

Acknowledgements

Thank you to my clients who inspire me every day with their stories of courage and persistence. You make me proud to be on your team.

Thank you to the amazing women who allowed me to share their stories in this book. Your experiences brought the messages to life.

Thank you to the men who support women, stand for them and champion them (and read books like these). Keep going. Your support matters.

Thank you to my production team and my cheer squad of supporters who helped me nurture this book into life. Your expertise, guidance and unwavering belief helped me get this out into the world.

Finally, thank you to my husband and mother for always being there. I cannot express how much your support means to me. And, most of all, thank you for graciously accepting my endless, mid-sentence interruptions of 'Sorry, can you hold that thought? I've just had an idea for the book. Gotta write it down.' You are my rocks.

First published in 2023 by BACCA House Press

A catalogue entry for this book is available from the National Library of Australia.

ISBN: 978-1-922764-32-4

Printed in Australia by McPherson's Printing
Book production and text design by Publish Central
Cover design by Publish Central and Pipeline Design

The paper this book is printed on is certified as environmentally friendly.

Click the provided QR code to access bonus material for this book.
(www.thegenderpenalty.com/bonuses)

Contents

Introduction

After two years of taking on extra responsibility, working overtime, managing and developing her peers – and, frankly, working at a level above her pay grade – Anne had had enough. It was time to secure her promotion and pay rise once and for all. She marched into her boss's office and tried one more time to get the raise she was promised – the one she deserved.

'What? He said no! Again??!!' This was the collective cry from the women in her coaching group. Anne was sharing her story with us and the women were having none of it. 'But you're already doing the job!' 'And you've been working twice as hard as everyone else.' 'It doesn't make any sense.'

And it didn't. Her boss had given her yet another excuse and Anne had heard them all. 'You're not ready yet.' 'We need to see more leadership skills, more confidence, more executive presence.' 'We don't have the budget but we think you're amazing and we'll look into it in the next financial year.' And my favourite, 'We've got a hiring freeze right now so we can't make any new appointments. It's from head office, our hands are tied.' Bah!

Anne was highly capable and committed, loyal and hard-working, deserving and diligent. Yet she was still overlooked, ignored and undervalued.

Anne's story is not unusual. You've likely heard it before. You may even be living it right now. Perhaps you've been skipped over for promotion because you weren't 'ready yet', or missed out on important assignments because you worked part-time. Or maybe you've been told you're lacking confidence – or you're too aggressive or too nice or too quiet or too direct. Agghhh! What's going on?

Since 2006, I've been working with women like Anne to help them fast-track their corporate careers and navigate the nuances of gender equality, in male-dominated environments. Through my 'Women at Work' masterclasses, coaching groups and keynote presentations, I've helped thousands of talented women build the confidence and clout to turn obstacles into opportunities and amplify their professional impact. But I wasn't always an advocate for gender equality. In fact, for a long time, I didn't understand what all the fuss was about.

The accidental feminist

I grew up believing women could do anything. My maternal grandmother was an industrious and entrepreneurial go-getter. As a young woman during the 1940s and '50s, her life got off to a traditional start. She got married young, had five children and was a stay-at-home wife, like most women of the time. But even in her homemaker role, my grandmother was building greenhouses, changing the oil in the car and driving a big Bedford truck around the neighbourhood. Her unconventional spirit defied the times. By her mid-forties, she had come out as a gay woman and, with the same independent spirit, went on to run a multitude of businesses, including a steakhouse, a pancake parlour, a milk bar and a plant wholesaler. My own mum, who raised my brother and me alone, was the most capable woman I knew. She could fix a dripping tap, program the VCR (that's old person speak for Netflix on big cassette tapes) and throw together a makeshift ballet costume, without batting an eye. No experience needed, no qualifications, no instructions – just pure intelligence, perseverance and a penchant for problem-solving.

I carried this independent, can-do spirit with me throughout my childhood, most of which was spent trailing my two closest cousins, Sharon and Paul. Sharon was three years older than me and Paul was six years older. Every day after school I would go around to their house, hanging around like a bad smell, waiting for Paul to finish his homework. Then it was play time. We would play cricket, tennis, basketball; sometimes just the two of us, sometimes with his friends. It was funny to watch his friends all come forward on the cricket pitch when 'the little girl' was batting, only to all spread out again after they witnessed my mean hook shot for the first time. I loved being underestimated. It was my secret weapon. If Paul had too much homework, I would stalk Sharon instead. With Sharon, we would bounce on the trampoline for hours, climb trees and make up competitive sport challenges for each other. And, yes, we always won, because that's what happens when you make up your own rules. You stack the odds for a win. Little did I know, it would be much harder to stack the odds as a grown woman.

It wasn't until I started my own business in 2006 that I had my first inkling that society treated women differently. That you didn't get to be on the field with the boys just because you expected to be, and that you couldn't just make up your own rules to win the game you were playing. And maybe, just maybe, the rules that were in place meant the game wasn't fair for women. I remember while completing my coaching diploma someone asked me what my coaching speciality was going to be. At the time, I wasn't sure. But I was sure what I was *not* going to be: a women's empowerment coach. It felt like every second person in my coaching school wanted to coach and empower women, and I couldn't figure out why. What was wrong with women? And why did so many of them need help? I didn't think I needed special help, so why did other women? It's important to note here that at the time I was footloose and fancy-free. I had just left my corporate job and started my own coaching and training business. With no mortgage, no kids, no husband and no commitments, I was able to work long hours, and travel at a moment's notice. I was ambitious and single-minded and thought success was an inside job. I made my own luck and created my own opportunities … weren't other women doing the same?

The answer took a while longer to crystallise, but crystallise it did. While I remained steadfast in my desire not to 'fix women', I did end up coaching a lot of them. I became a specialist in communication – helping leaders build influence, engagement and interpersonal impact to fast-track their corporate careers. And, without realising it, I began moonlighting as a women's empowerment coach. Even though I was coaching both men and women to have greater communication and leadership impact, the obstacles faced by my female clients were very different from those faced by the men – especially as they became more senior. A pattern began to emerge.

My female clients reported challenges in being seen, being heard and being valued. They complained of being talked over in a meeting, being ignored in a group setting, having to justify, explain or defend their ideas, and of having their ideas appropriated by others who were louder, more bold or more confident. My male clients, on the other hand, focused more on building empathy and emotional intelligence (EQ) skills, and rarely on being seen as a leader, being taken seriously or being heard. The more I worked with these talented and dedicated women, the more I realised being highly competent and hardworking was not enough for these women to get ahead. They were just as talented, driven and capable as the men, but they faced invisible obstacles that their male counterparts simply did not. They faced what I came to call the gender penalty.

In response to some of the challenges women were describing in my one-on-one coaching sessions, I began delivering keynotes and workshops on credible communication – how to make your value visible. This was an attempt to reach more women and equip them with communication tools and strategies to be seen, heard and valued as the talented professionals they were. My focus was on ensuring they were taken seriously and exuding that all-too-often elusive executive presence that stood between them and their next promotion. Women couldn't get enough of my presentations and workshops on this topic.

Still, to this day, my Credible Communication presentation remains one of my most sought after. My accidental feminism was in full flight. I was empowering women and it was about to get a lot more serious.

Even as I continued to struggle with the idea that women shouldn't need this kind of special help (to 'fix' them), more and more of my clients were asking me to support their women leaders. And I knew from my coaching and keynote work that women actually did need help. Not because they weren't good enough, but because the system they worked in was not set up to support their success. That's when I embraced my role in helping women. That's when I finally understood what all the fuss was about. I made the decision: I was all in. And at the risk of perpetuating the myth that women needed special support to be better leaders, I developed my flagship, award-winning Women at Work program, aimed at helping women navigate a male-dominated leadership landscape and fast-track their career success. The many conversations, stories and experiences from working with these women are what this book is based on.

Why I wrote this book

I want to give you what my female clients have been asking for, for years: strategies to build confidence, tools for improving communication impact, ways to make their value visible, the ability to say no and hold boundaries and the tools to navigate working motherhood with grace. At the same time, I want to ensure you understand the broader context of why women are struggling with these issues, and what they do about them.

> When women think issues are theirs alone, they tend to personalise them, but once they know these issues are felt collectively, they start to mobilise against them.

This shift in thinking is critical in giving women the clarity and conviction to both address the issues in the moment and lobby for systemic change in the long run.

In this book, I want to remind you of your brilliance and the desperate need to have more women like you in our leadership ranks. I want to redistribute the burden of change from women's shoulders back to the workplace, and equip you with strategies and tools to navigate the current male-dominated workplace, at the same time. In the process, I want to normalise the experience of work for women, to help them know that they are not alone. This is about understanding the conditioning that has created our current world of work, the courage required to make a change and the practical strategies that will get you there. But, most importantly, I want to inspire the next generation of strong female voices – the voices of women who will courageously speak their truth, hold their ground and ask for what they want, at any stage of their career.

And while this book is to help you get what you want at work, it's also so much more than that. It's about opening the doors for more women, sisters, mothers, daughters, aunties, grandmothers, colleagues and friends. It's about normalising the presence of women in power and authority, and harnessing the brilliance of the diverse thinking, experiences and backgrounds only women can offer. To put simply, this book is a call to women to use their voices and value to build a better world for women at work – and that's better for everybody.

Who this book is for

This book is for you if you want to understand how to navigate your career, as a woman in the working world, dominated by the male leadership lens. If you want to know how to stand out without stepping on toes, how to get what you want without compromising who you are, and how to make your mark without becoming someone you're not, you're in the right place.

The strategies in this book are for women in management and leadership roles in male-dominated environments. Maybe you're from finance, engineering, IT or construction but, regardless of your industry, you've been around long enough to have bumped into the invisible barriers of being a woman in a male-dominated workplace. You've realised that the advice of 'work harder' or 'be better' just doesn't work for women as it does for men. Whether you're a mid-level manager wanting to grow your influence and impact, or a senior executive looking to shake up the industry, this book is a critical resource for normalising your experiences in the workforce and providing practical solutions to progress your career – for yourself and for the sisterhood.

It's also important to note that not every woman experiences the gender penalties in the same way. Some will experience more penalties at particular stages of their career and others less so. I'm also not covering intersectional areas of discrimination for women arising from race, colour, class, nationality, ability, geography or sexual identity, in order to keep the ideas and the solutions tight and targeted.

Another thing to note about this book is that when I talk about the typical behaviours of men and women, they are simply that: typical, common behaviours of cis-gender men and women. You'll note I am also referencing 'men' and 'women', and not the full range of gender identities. Again, my intent is to keep the focus of the book to these two, specific gendered experiences.

The game of work – do we adapt the play or advance the game?

Women, in general, work differently to men. Women bring specific skills and strengths to the table that add power, compassion and efficacy to the world of work. The problem is that the game of work was built by men, for men, and the rules that serve to support men, end up sidelining women. So when women stand up and speak out to offer their skills, who is really listening?

Throughout this book I use the analogy of work as a game. Not because I think we should be 'playing political games' but because that's how men view the world of work; like a game to be played. And while you might not want to think of work as a game to be played, the reality is the game is already underway, whether we like it or not. And if we want to change the game for women, we need to get ourselves onto the field. And this is where it gets interesting ...

Do we help women to adapt their behaviours so they can win the game currently being played ('fixing women'), or do we help women to advance the game in the long run so the game is better for everyone ('fixing the workforce')? With so many self-help books on the market advocating for the two different approaches (*Lean In* by Sheryl Sandberg and *Stop Fixing Women* by Catherine Fox come to mind as two classic examples), it is hard to know which solution is best. The answer for each of us is different but one thing is true: combining strategies from both camps will give you the best chance of winning your own game at work, however you need to play it. With every penalty, you can make a choice. You can double-down and push through to advance the game for the long-term, or you can choose your battles and pull back to adapt the play in the moment. For example, you might change the way you speak in a meeting to cut through a sea of strong voices – this is adapting the play in the moment, to stay in the game. Or you might lobby to get the meeting format changed so that everyone gets a chance to speak – this is advancing the game in the long run. Both choices are valid and both are needed to keep us moving forward.

And for those of you in the 'stop fixing women' camp, I hear you. Truly. And I really wish this strategy alone was enough. But it's not. As a practical person, I'm focused on strategies that work. Sometimes that means, as women, we need to adapt our behaviours in the moment, even if we feel we shouldn't have to. This is not about asking you to be someone you are not. (No-one should have to change their character to get ahead at work.) However, everyone needs to change how they are willing to behave, if what they are doing is not getting the results they want. It's called 'behavioural flexibility' and it's important for professional survival. It's like visiting a foreign country and choosing to speak the language of that country so you can be better understood. You're not giving up your passport, or your identity; you're just speaking in a language that the other person can understand. You are adapting your behaviour to get a better outcome for yourself. Yes, you can cross your arms and stubbornly refuse to be the one 'who has to change' but you may have to wait a while for the others to learn your language. It's always easier to be bilingual.

In the game of work, women are still in the minority in leadership and executive roles. We are outnumbered and so most men don't 'speak our language'. Men are the dominant culture that sets the rules, upholds the rules and wins by the rules (whether consciously or not). Just as their rules are often invisible to us, our behaviours are often invisible to them. This isn't because they don't think we matter, but because there are not enough of us normalising our leadership and corporate choices to make our presence a legitimate part of the game. Weirdly, it's not about us, but it does affect us. We need to adapt to their game, so we can be seen, heard and respected enough to win. This is how we get off the bench, onto the field and eventually inside the club house to change the rules.

We know many of the issues women face at work are a result of systemic bias, inherited corporate cultures and years of conditioning to subscribe to male and female roles. We know these issues are not the result of women's choices or behaviours alone, but rather how society views these choices and behaviours. We know women are not the problem, and it's the workforce that needs fixing, but that doesn't stop us being part of the solution. We need to both adapt the play and advance the game. This book offers the pathway for both.

The game of work is a problem for women that can't be solved by solutions for men. Women need a new set of skills to navigate the leadership landscape in their own way and on their own terms. It's time to change the play and the game.

The gender penalties

In the game of work, unwritten rules create invisible obstacles that penalise women at work and sideline us from the main game. I call these obstacles the 'gender penalties' because they break the unspoken rules that work for men, but penalise women. The five penalties covered in this book include:

1. **The Confidence penalty**

   The rule: Leaders need to show confidence.

   - Men who show confidence are seen as competent.
   - Women who show confidence are seen as arrogant.

2. **The Communication penalty**

   The rule: Leaders need to speak up and have a voice.

   - Men who speak up are visible and valued.
   - Women who speak up are interrupted, talked over or ignored.

3. **The Boasting penalty**

   The rule: Leaders need to sell their strengths.

   - Men who talk about their achievements appear accomplished.
   - Women who talk about their achievements appear boastful.

4. **The Strength penalty**

   The rule: Leaders need to be strong.

   - Men who are strong are seen as assertive.
   - Women who are strong are seen as aggressive.

5. **The Motherhood penalty**

   The rule: Leaders need to be full-time and committed.

   - Men who have children are available and seen as more responsible.
   - Women who have children are seen as less available and less committed.

These penalties not only create hidden obstacles but also work to keep women invisible in the workplace and sidelined from the main game. Their achievements can be ignored and their impact compromised. This book is all about showing you how you can overcome these penalties, moving from invisible to invaluable as you amplify your impact in your workplace. Of course, the penalties outlined here are not the only ones women face at work; however these are the ones that come up time and again in the research, and in my masterclasses and coaching conversations. Once we unpack the strategies for each penalty and supplement them with the power plays coming later, the type of penalty you face as a woman, will matter a whole lot less. You'll have the skills and tools you need to win the game of work.

Getting the most out of this book

In keeping with the metaphor of the game of work, I've broken the book into three parts: 'The state of play', 'The gender penalties' and 'The power plays to advance the game'.

In part I, I cover the current corporate context. What does the leadership landscape look like for women? What's going on for women at work? Why are women facing invisible obstacles despite being over-qualified? Why do the solutions for men create problems for women? And why are we still playing this outdated game in the first place?

In part II, I deep dive into the five gender penalties – the Confidence, Communication, Boasting, Strength and Motherhood penalties. I explore what these penalties are and how they are currently playing out for women at work. I cover the rules women are expected to follow and the penalty they face when they do, as well as the stories from the field, showcasing how women have overcome these obstacles and turned them into opportunities. I end each chapter with practical strategies on how to adapt the play in the moment, and win the game of work for your career success. I also provide a handy Playbook Checklist that summarises the pre-game attitudes and on-field actions to get your head in the game and keep your hands on the ball.

And finally, in part III, we wrap up with the Power Plays for advancing the game. Every game has a way to fast-track success – whether it's access to a penalty shootout in overtime or access to super powers when you hit a bonus level in a computer game. The game of work also offers ways to gain access to super powers to change the game in the long term. In the chapters in this part, I cover how to change the game you're playing to make it work better for women (and men). I explore having the courage to challenge the conditioning that keeps us stuck in the old game, and the power to start where you are and challenge the norms you encounter. I discuss the power of amplifying others and braving the backlash in service of creating the new game, with new rules and a better outcome for all.

To get the most out of this book, you can treat it like a buffet or a banquet. You can skip to the bit you need, when you need it (like a buffet, where you can have dessert first – don't judge me), or you can read the whole thing from start to finish like a delicious seven-course meal. Either way, you'll get the nutrients you need, when you need them. And by the end of this book, you'll be more able to turn career obstacles into opportunities and win the game of work. Let's begin.

Notes

PART I

THE STATE OF PLAY

In order to win the game of work, we need to know the state of play on the field. Games are won as much through strategy as they are through skill, so we need to take stock. What are the opportunities and threats, the strengths of the players and the conditions of the competition? We need to understand the context that creates the game we're playing and, ultimately, determines what's needed to win.

In the chapters in this part, I explore what's going on for women at work. I celebrate the power of women in the workforce to highlight that talented women are not the exception to the rule but the norm, the baseline. I also explore where you are in the game of work – what your personal brand is and what you need to focus on to get to the next step in your career.

I take you through the metaphors of life for men and women, and show how they shape your professional impact at work. This helps in understanding why the game of work feels different for men and women. I look at how the curse of conditioning has further widened this difference, and hoodwinked us all into playing roles that pre-determine our pathways and potential, with or without our permission.

And, finally, I explore the role of backlash, bias and men in holding women's stereotypes in place and keeping the current game in play. And once we're done, you'll likely never see the workplace the same way again. And that will be a good thing. I promise.

Chapter 1

What's going on for women at work?

Women have been conditioned by so many aspects of society to think, believe and act in certain ways to fit the female stereotype. Unfortunately, the traditional female stereotype doesn't fit the traditional leadership stereotype (because it's based on men). That's the problem. The more women try to fit into the current leadership stereotype, the more they have to move outside of the female stereotype – and the more they experience social backlash.

Women in Western society have generally been conditioned to be modest, humble, helpful, supportive and caring. This is what we expect from 'good girls', who are 'well mannered' and 'play nicely with others'. The trouble is this conditioning is not authoritative. It's not commanding. It shows no 'executive presence' or corporate credibility, and it doesn't fit the leadership style we have come to expect.

So, women are encouraged to go against these stereotypical behaviours, and told to take charge, speak up, be more assertive … and then they get whacked. Society takes a swing at them with the big old backlash bat and knocks out their confidence – and any remaining chutzpah for good measure. This reinforces the value of staying small, being silent, downplaying strengths and accommodating the needs of others. Just like a good girl should. Sigh.

Women are sidelined from the game of work because they are playing by the wrong set of rules. When they play by men's rules, they get punished for not being 'ladylike', and when they play by women's rules, they get punished for not being 'leaderlike'. Damned if you do, and damned if you don't!

This is an issue because men are still the majority when it comes to power and leadership in Western countries, and so they become the unconscious benchmark against which women are measured. And, therefore, women all too often come up lacking; seen as not hard enough even though warmth is the winner, not loud enough when a whisper is all that's required, not bold enough when caution is the right choice. Women are not better or worse, they are just different. But when held against a model that doesn't fit them, they are seen as lacking. We need to stop seeing women as being different from the 'norm', and start embracing their difference *as* the norm – the expanded, more complete norm.

The female factor

Emily was the general manager of logistics in a global company. While changing industries from heavy manufacturing to commodities, she noticed that the safety standards in her new industry were not at the same level as the heavy manufacturing industry. She knew that improving the safety focus in her company alone would not change the industry safety challenges overall, so she reached out to like-minded leaders within the industry who shared the same values and aspiration to make a difference (for their own companies and every participant in that supply chain). She did what women have been doing for centuries and pulled people together to effect change collectively. She mobilised people from different companies (competitors, no less), formed an industry safety network, and together with these like-minded leaders, created new standards, and lifted the tide of safety standards across her industry.

Her boss asked, 'Why are you doing this? Isn't this taking you away from focusing on your own KPIs? Why are you so passionate about this matter?' Emily was adamant – the only way to win individually on this issue was to win collectively across the supply chain. And she was right. Not only did she reach a new level of safety standards in her own company, along with her colleagues, but she also raised the bar for the whole industry. The industry safety network (which she chaired for two years) still exists, and she is still continuing her vision and leveraging the legacy. She didn't do what was expected, popular or normal; she did what she felt was right. What was needed. What would make a real difference, for all. She leveraged the female factor.

When women work differently, it's tempting to focus only on what women lack and need to improve to be seen as 'leaderlike'. But it's more inspiring, empowering and important to instead recognise and amplify the skills they already bring to the table. This is not to say how much *better* women are than men, but to show how much better the world could be if we honoured the strengths that women bring, as we do for men.

Let's get clear on the talents and strengths women bring to the game of work, why their leadership style matters, and what happens when we embrace more of this.

> When we celebrate the positive impact of women, we see how vital they are in boardrooms, on executive committees, in parliament, in leadership, in community groups, in industry forums, in media, in academia, on stages, on screens and in all important conversations that affect our lives. And maybe, just maybe, we inspire more women to come forward and share their brilliance.

Women are exemplary leaders

Women embrace a transformational leadership style over a transactional leadership style (and not necessarily because they were born to, but often because they were conditioned to). A transformational style is collaborative, conscientious and caring, whereas a transactional leadership style is more controlling, commanding and competitive. Women who embrace transformational leadership generally care about their teams, and engage them on a deep personal level, with empathy, empowerment and equity. It's what engages hearts and minds and engenders loyalty and trust. (And no this doesn't mean that men don't care about their teams or engage them with empathy as well; it just means, on average, more women than men exhibit this kind of leadership style.)

In his book *Why Do So Many Incompetent Men Become Leaders?* (yes, that is the real title), Tomas Chamorro-Premuzic describes results from a meta-analysis of 45 leadership and gender studies. The findings show that women are more effective than men in leading their teams and organisations. Also, the leadership traits where women excelled were more positively correlated to effective leadership, whereas the leadership traits where men excelled were more negatively correlated with effective leadership. As Chamorro-Premuzic puts it,

> *Where women are different, they perform better. Where men are different, they perform worse.*

For me, this is not about women being inherently better leaders than men; however, it is about women being socialised to embody a leadership style that is more effective. Men who embrace this same style are also effective, but in general men are conditioned to embrace a transactional leadership style instead.

And to make this more granular, let's review some research by US management and leadership consultants Zenger and Folkman, who have been studying the characteristics of leadership effectiveness for over

30 years. In a survey of 7280 leaders in 2011, they found women rate higher in overall leadership effectiveness than their male counterparts, with the greatest gap evident at the highest executive levels. Zenger and Folkman then broke effective leadership down into the top 16 competencies top leaders exemplify most. These competencies were:

· takes initiative

· practises self-development

· displays high integrity and honesty

· drives for results

· develops others

· inspires and motivates others

· builds relationships

· works collaboratively and with the team

· establishes stretch goals

· champions change

· solves problems and analyses issues

· communicates powerfully and prolifically

· connects the group to the outside world

· innovates

· displays technical or professional expertise

· develops strategic perspective.

In 15 out of the 16 competencies, women rated higher – yes, 15 out of 16. And here's the kicker: two of these competencies have always been associated with typically 'male' leadership characteristics – taking initiative and driving for results. Incidentally, the only competency men rated higher on was 'develops strategic perspective' – and only just (51 male mean percentile versus 49 female mean percentile. (Even so, is it any wonder they are still leading the game?)

In their 2020 *Harvard Business Review* research article, 'Women are better leaders during a crisis', Zenger and Folkman also highlighted that women were more effective in leading through the pandemic, based on an analysis of 360-degree assessments.

And UN Women agrees. In their 2020 policy brief 'COVID-19 and women's leadership: From an effective response to building back better', they described the leadership styles of women as 'more collective than individual, more collaborative than competitive, and more coaching than commanding' – that's transformational leadership in a nutshell. The UN Women brief lauded female leaders for showing greater effectiveness and inclusiveness in managing the COVID-19 crisis and delivering transparent and compassionate communication of important public health information. The policy brief also highlighted the opportunities to 'build back better' in a post-COVID world through more inclusion and support of women leaders.

Added to this are the findings from McKinsey & Company in their report 'Women Matter 2: Female leadership, a competitive edge for the future'. The report looked at how often men and women apply the nine leadership traits found to positively affect organisational performance. Women were found to apply five of these behaviours more than men:

- people development
- expectation and rewards
- role model
- inspiration
- participative decision-making.

Whereas men adopted only two behaviours more than women:

- control and corrective action
- individualistic decision-making.

There it is again: transformational versus transactional leadership – a focus on collaboration and care versus command and control. This report from McKinsey & Company was published in 2008, but we're still struggling to have the strengths of female leadership acknowledged. (And if you're keeping count, the two remaining leadership behaviours of intellectual stimulation and efficient communication were equally used by both genders.) Again, all of this is not to say that women are born better leaders than men, but that their socialised conditioning invites them to embrace the traits and characteristics that happen to make great leaders. The research highlights that the lack of women in leadership, authority and power is not due to a lack of leadership competence. The research is clear; women are exemplary leaders.

Women's strengths are needed *right now*

It's not just corporate leadership roles where women excel (even while in the minority); they also have strengths in other traditionally male-dominated areas. Did you know that trains driven by female drivers have lower maintenance costs? Turns out female drivers are softer on the brakes, which creates less wear and tear on the trains. The same goes for female truck drivers, as told to me by the CEO of one of Australia's largest automotive companies. Another HR director shared a similar story, telling me that their female waste collection truck drivers are more careful when lining up to the bins on the curb (and so spend less time reversing and correcting). As a result, they are more on time than their male counterparts. Then there are the multiple research findings that report that female police officers are especially effective at defusing high tension situations in the field by relying on emotional sensitivity, not brute strength.[1]

See the following breakout box for more lists of reasons women's strengths are needed right now.

Women bring in the dosh

Companies with a larger number of senior women produce better financial performance.[2]

Companies with more women on executive committees bring in more revenue.[3]

Women improve engagement

11,434 adults surveyed by Gallup showed a 6 per cent higher engagement rate of employees led by females.[4]

Women raise the standards

Boards with more women are more ethical.[5]

Female entrepreneurs tend to be more risk averse but produce better long-term results.[6]

Women share the credit and take responsibility for more failure.[7]

The mere presence of women police officers reduces the use of force among other officers.[8]

Women make men better

Balancing a team of men with women lifts the collective intelligence of the group.[9] (Now I'm not saying women are smarter per se, but the clever folks at MIT in the United States where this study was completed hypothesised that it was because women were better at reading social cues and showed greater social sensitivity, which helped everyone be their very best.)

We need the talents of women and we need them now. Not to over-shadow men, but to walk in line with men. Diversity is the only game that really delivers. And in order to get there, we need to right the imbalance.

> We need more women in authority. We need more women in senior roles in organisations, industries and communities. We need diversity of thinking, experience and perspective. But mostly we need to normalise the presence of women in power.

I want to hear a female voice come over the loudspeaker on my next plane flight and not be surprised when she introduces herself as the captain. I want our presence in the world to be visible, valued and expected. Just like men.

Break conditioning and become courageous

Having more women in leadership broadens the leadership bench-mark. Women are their own type of leader, not an offshoot of the male model. We are our own model. And combined with the best traits of male leadership, we can expand the base model to be even better.

To broaden these leadership benchmarks and be valued in our own right, we need to break out of our conditioning and embrace the courage to start pushing back on society's expectations. How we do this depends on where we are in our careers and what we personally need to work on to take the next step. While this book covers the gender penalties that keep too many women stuck on the bench and the power plays to even the playing field, it's important to know how you are personally being affected and where you are in your career right now. What professional brand do you have as a player on the field? What behaviours are keeping you stuck or helping you succeed? What impact will your skills have on the game at play? And what does it mean for your career outcomes?

The Gendered Career Ladder

This journey can be mapped on my Gendered Career Ladder, which describes various stages in a woman's career – as shown in the following figure. While the ladder is presented in a linear fashion, women's careers are anything but. You may find yourself moving up and down the rungs as your circumstances change. New roles, bosses, companies or industries can all have an impact on where you find yourself at any point in time. The important thing to remember is that you can also move yourself up and down this ladder by your own efforts.

The Gendered Career Ladder for women

BRAND	BEHAVIOURS	IMPACT	RESULTS	
Invaluable	do the Impossible things	Amplified	Elevated	COURAGEOUS
Credible	do the Hard things	Valued	Taken seriously	COURAGEOUS
Competent	do the Right things	Known	Taken for granted	CONDITIONED
Compliant	do All the things	Compromised	Taken for a ride	CONDITIONED
Invisible	do Anything	Absent	Ignored	CONDITIONED

Let's review the rungs, starting from the bottom up:

- **Invisible:** Unseen and unheard, you're pretty much invisible. You're still establishing yourself, so you do anything. Your efforts are unfocused and so your impact is absent. Your value is ignored. Ouch! Time to level up quick smart.

- **Compliant:** Agreeable, amenable, the people pleaser. You do a lot for others (and I mean *a lot*). You struggle to say no and are therefore taken for a ride. People get used to your compliance and congeniality and start to expect you to do everything they ask. Your impact at work is compromised because you are busy doing unimportant tasks that are probably not even your job. Stop it! Get those assertive skills going and get out of there ASAP.

- **Competent:** Capable, committed, the backbone. You work on the right things. You are building skills on boundary setting in order to keep on top of your work. Your hard work and contribution is acknowledged and you are relied on to keep the place running. Perhaps you're even too important to promote? You're so good at making the department look good that your commitment is taken for granted. You need a promotion and you need it yesterday!

- **The tipping point:** At the Competent stage, you've reached the tipping point. The strategies you have employed so far are aimed at navigating workforce conditioning – adapting the play to stay on the field. You have been steadily overcoming the gender penalties of how women are expected to play the game of work. You've proven that women are equally competent players and deserve to be on the field too. Now it's time to advance the game. It's time to use your courage to break out of the conditioning and start changing the game. It's time to elevate your outcomes and amplify your impact. Let the real game begin.

- **Credible:** Strategic, focused, the deliverer. You work on what you need to work on if it's on your critical path. You have the hard conversations and are prepared to push back on others in order to keep yourself focused and able to deliver. You are taken seriously by others and your impact is valued. Keep going. You're on track. Next stop is the top, baby!

- **Invaluable:** Empowered, respected, the amplifier. You are a pioneer for women. You have done the impossible and continue to pave the way for other women. You are making a massive difference in the world and are respected and revered by those around you. Your outcome is elevated and your impact amplified. Because you celebrate the power and purpose of people, programs, industries and communities, your reach in this world is infinite. You have arrived! Congratulations. You are living into your full potential and bringing others with you. Go you good thing!

Once you know where you are on the Gendered Career Ladder you can easily see the path forward. Is this about navigating the conditioning or having the courage to break out of it? How quickly can you learn the invisible rules and navigate the gender penalties as they arise? Will you focus more on adapting the play or advancing the game? The choice is yours, and the rest of this book is all about providing more information, tips and strategies in these areas to help you choose. For now, the journey to becoming an invaluable player has begun.

Now we've explored what's going on for women at work, why we need more of them on the field and where we currently are in our own careers, it's time to learn what game we're actually playing and why women are stuck on the bench.

Chapter 2

What game are we playing?

'I know it's only morning tea time, but that last segment of the workshop has just explained my whole corporate career as a woman. All these years, I've been playing the wrong game. If I learn nothing else for the rest of the day, this has still been the best training of my corporate career to date!' This comment came from a participant in my Women at Work masterclass on our way to morning tea. (FYI: she learnt heaps more. ☺) She had just been let into the best kept secret in town – a secret that most men and women don't know. A secret that has created thriving conditions for the gender penalties to grow for eons. It's the metaphor of life.

In 1993, sociolinguist, professor and author Suzette Haden Elgin introduced us to the idea of an operating metaphor in her book *Genderspeak: Men, women, and the gentle art of verbal self-defense.* Elgin highlighted the way men and women largely relate to their lives through the lens of different operating metaphors. These operating metaphors act like a guide for how to live your life. They drive the fundamental decisions, behaviours and choices you make every day. When asked to finish the sentence, 'Life is like a …' (You just said 'box of chocolates!' didn't you? I see you!) men said 'team sport' and women said 'classroom'.

I remember when I first heard this metaphor. It just made so much sense. Everything fell into place and I realised why I was getting frustrated about why men didn't seem to 'care as much' or didn't take things 'seriously enough' or weren't 'doing things right' (according to my standards). Finally, the answer to a question I hadn't even dared to formulate emerged. I was in the 'classroom' trying to be perfect and most men were in a 'team sport' trying to win the playoffs. So, let's look more closely at what it means to be in these two metaphors for life and how it impacts the way we play the game of work.

The traditional classroom – being a 'good girl'

In the traditional classroom metaphor, we treat work like we're at school. You do the work, you study for the test, you help your class-mates, you put your hand up and wait your turn. You work hard and then you move up a grade. You never cheat. If you do the right thing, you'll get the result. It's about who you are. Everything is personal.

When transferred to the workplace, many women continue to think that success comes from performance. That is, if you do the right thing and work hard, be diligent, take on more responsibility, get more qual-ifications and follow the rules, the value of the work will speak for itself (and no need to brag). Opportunities will abound and promotions will naturally follow. (Spoiler alert: they don't.)

The team sport – being the 'best player'

In the traditional team sport metaphor, men treat work like it's a game. And they want to win. In order to win, you need to prove your worth to the coach and be continually picked for the team. You need to showcase your strengths, be heard, be seen and be better than the competition. Once you're on the field, you need to do whatever it takes to win – steal a base, bend the rules, strategise your play against the opponents' weaknesses. It's about how you play the game. And once it's done, it's done. Game over. Beers on. Nothing is personal.

When transferred to the workplace, many men continue to think success comes from the strategy of the game. It's a competition of who can be seen by the right people, in the right way, at the right time, to get ahead. They make sure their achievements are visible, their ideas are heard and their strengths are always on display. If you don't play full out, it's your fault you're not winning, right?

This means, at work, women are generally working and waiting, missing out on jobs, pay, credit and opportunities, while men are striving and strategic, pushing forward, taking risks and grabbing opportunities.

> **Women are in the classroom developing capabilities, and men are on the sporting field positioning their performance.**

Even just thinking about the kind of uniform you would wear at school versus in sports adds to the image of the metaphors. For sports, your clothes are loose, flexible, durable and fit for purpose. They allow you to fall over, scuff your knees, get grubby and play full out to win. A school uniform is clean and tidy, tucked in, buttoned up, primped and preened to within an inch of its life. No room for breaking out of the mould here. It's a uniform that tells you to fall in line, not play flat out.

The curse of conditioning

It's important to note that men and women don't subscribe to these life metaphors because of a genetic disposition to do so. It's not because men are genetically better at sports (even if research has proven that men are physiologically able to throw further than women) and women are better at school. These life metaphors actually exist because men and women have been conditioned to behave in certain ways in accordance with their traditional gender stereotype.

In 2005, psychologist Dr Janet Shibley Hyde of the University of Wisconsin–Madison analysed 46 meta-analyses (studies of multiple studies) that were conducted over the previous 20 years. What she found showed that men and women were basically the same when it came to personality, cognitive ability and leadership. Gender differences that did exist were more to do with context and conditioning than inbuilt preferences, and they had a tendency to 'fluctuate with age, growing smaller or larger at different times in the life span'. Any differences were, therefore, not necessarily stable.

Hyde noted a few exceptions to her 'gender similarities hypothesis', including the fact that men could 'throw farther than women'. Yep. And in another twist, one study showed that when men and women knew their identities were not being recorded in the results, they acted in opposition to their gender conditioning. It turns out that women were more aggressive and men were more passive. Now this doesn't mean that women 'were aggressive' and men 'were passive', but simply that they were more aggressive and passive, respectively, than they would usually dare demonstrate when not trying to fit into the gender mould. We are desperate to be ourselves, but society struggles to see beyond the conditioned expectation and puts great pressure in holding us there.

What's your score?

So what's your score? How much have you been conditioned to be in the classroom or on the sporting field? Put a tick next to each item that describes you and let's find out.

Where did you score the most ticks? In the classroom or the team sport? How has this affected your career to date? What have you noticed is working or not working for you? What needs to change and what needs to stay the same?

Classroom	Team sports
☐ I play by the rules	☐ I bend the rules
☐ I want to cooperate	☐ I want to compete
☐ I share credit	☐ I take credit
☐ I help others at a cost to myself	☐ I put myself first
☐ I do everything right	☐ I do the right things
☐ I downplay my strengths	☐ I upsell my strengths
☐ I take blame	☐ I avoid blame
☐ I bruise easily	☐ I bounce back
☐ I take it personally	☐ I make it playful
☐ Everything is serious	☐ Everything is a game
☐ I accommodate others	☐ I stand firm in my own agenda
☐ I say yes	☐ I say find someone else
☐ I do thorough work	☐ I do only what's needed
☐ I step out of the spotlight	☐ I step into the spotlight
☐ Failure is embarrassing	☐ Failure is necessary
☐ Being honest is a non-negotiable	☐ Bending the truth is par for the course

What's your style?

Dr Deborah Tannen, a professor of linguistics at Georgetown University in Washington, has been studying the influence of linguistic style on conversations and human relationships for over 40 years. Since the 1990s, she has extended this research into the world of work. Her findings help to further explain what game we are really playing and why the game feels so different for men and women. Professor Tannen sheds light on some interesting observed (and conditioned) differences in how men and women communicate in the workplace. This supports the operating metaphors (classroom versus team sports) and how they are playing out at work.

In her book *Talking from 9 to 5. Women and men at work: Language, sex and power*, Professor Tannen describes women's conditioned communication patterns as co-operative. Women, generally, aim to connect. They want to minimise status differences and stay equal to others. They will ask more questions and communicate more indirectly as a way to elevate the status of others and not overshadow them or take the spotlight. They use modesty as an influence tool and apologies as a ritual for connection and concern, and as a way to save face for others. They also take pushback and debate as a personal affront and avoid it accordingly. Women are conditioned to be amenable.

Tannen highlighted that men, on the other hand, generally take a competitive approach. They aim to compete and to maintain a high-status position. They communicate more directly, asking fewer questions and elevating themselves over others. They influence through confidence and see apologies as a loss of status. They routinely engage in rigorous debate and opposition, seeing it as part of the game and a way to win – and then shrugging off any disagreements and moving on. Men are conditioned to be authoritative.

The following table highlights the different conditioning between men and women.

	Women are conditioned to	Men are conditioned to
Communicate	Indirectly	Directly
Ask	More	Less
Elevate	Others	Self
Engage	Co-operatively	Competitively
Minimise	Certainty	Doubt
Maximise	Modesty	Confidence
Apologise	Often	Rarely
Push back	Sparingly	Routinely
Step	Out of the spotlight	Into the spotlight
Interrupt	To add to the conversation	To redirect the conversation

Isn't it fascinating how aligned the conditioned communication choices are with the metaphor of the classroom and the team sports? Is it any wonder men are so good at playing this game? They have been training for it all their lives.

Understanding why you might be sitting in the classroom and not on the sporting field provides insight into why some things will be supporting your career and some things will be sabotaging it. These aspects come about not because of how capable you are but because the things you value in the classroom are not necessarily valued on the field ... yet. As discussed in the previous chapter, many things about being in the classroom will move society forward and we need to honour and protect these strengths. *But* it is no use being in the classroom on your own! This often puts you on the sidelines of the main game – where no-one is watching, listening or taking note of the progress you're making or the potential you're offering.

> **If you don't have the respect or attention of the world in arenas that matter most, you are not living into your full potential. You'll miss the opportunity to advance the game and blend the benefits of the classroom and the sporting field. And this blend is the ultimate win–win for all.**

This chapter has outlined how the real game being played is the team sport. I've covered why women are playing by a different set of rules (in the classroom) and why their value is often invisible and they are left on the bench. In the next chapter, I explore why changing our behaviours to play the team sport is getting us off the bench, but still causing us to foul. Once you understand these invisible forces, you can start to make informed choices about how much you want to engage with the game being played and how much you want to lobby to change the game altogether.

Chapter 3

Why are we getting fouled?

Mary was a vibrant, bright, ambitious, high-performing young woman on the fast track to success within her company. She was being groomed for senior leadership through constant support and developmental feedback. She loved the opportunity to grow and develop, and took all the feedback very seriously. Over months of support to be more this and less that, and do more this and less that, and say this and not that, she started to notice a disturbing pattern. The feedback was contradictory and, quite frankly, confusing.

At first, she was told she was too quiet, too invisible, too hidden. No surprises there – she had her head down in the 'classroom', and was focused on doing great work. She was encouraged to speak up, share her opinions, make herself heard and demonstrate 'executive presence'. In other words, get off the bench and come play on the field like the rest of the team. However, when she started coming out of her shell and sharing her opinions, sometimes pushing back and standing her ground and telling people what she thought, she began to get a different type of feedback. She was told she was annoying people and she was in danger of putting people offside – that she was now too strong, too direct and too much for people. She needed to tone it down.

Mary was confused. She had done as she was asked and got off the bench. She moved from the classroom to the sporting field, only to get fouled once the game was in play. She didn't understand what she had done wrong. She was playing like the others, but somehow it wasn't translating properly. She didn't know what to do. Stay quiet and be benched, or speak up and be fouled? And, more importantly, why was she the only one attracting a foul, when her behaviours were the same as the rest of the team?

The game of work is often a problem for women that can't be solved by solutions meant for men.

Social backlash

When women try to apply well-meaning advice (that usually works for men), it often backfires on them. They get fouled. Confused and increasingly uncertain, they are left to wonder what they've done wrong. They wonder why adopting the 'leadership behaviours' that men adopt doesn't get the same results as it does for men. Enter social backlash.

Social backlash is the whistle that blows when you are playing out of bounds. It's society's negative reinforcement when you are not playing by the rules. It's what earns you the foul. And in the game of work, the whistle blows for women not because we are not playing by the rules of work, but because we are not playing by the rules of our gender. The rules of being 'leaderlike' are at odds with the rules for being 'ladylike'. This is because traditionally more men have been in leadership roles, so we tend to associate 'leaderlike' behaviours with male behaviours.

When women take on advice to be more 'leaderlike', they are not seen to take on leadership behaviours, but the behaviours of men. As a result, they face a social backlash because they are not acting like 'typical' women. When men are told they need to speak up, be more visible and put their ideas on the table, they can simply do so and the job is done. When a woman is told the same thing and attempts to execute in the same way, she faces a different experience. Rather than being seen as assertive her behaviour is labelled aggressive; instead of being seen as confident, she is seen as arrogant. It's not about the behaviour, it's about who's doing the behaviour.

It's like dabbing. When my stepdaughter Sienna was 10, she went through a phase of dabbing. Dabbing (if you're not a parent or somehow missed the trend) is when you make a certain move with both arms after you've achieved something cool. It kind of looks like you're sneezing into your sleeve while your back arm goes out straight like you're doing a dance move. When the craze was at its height, kids were dabbing to each other on the streets, dabbing after shooting a goal, and dabbing after flipping a plastic bottle that landed the right end up. They dabbed a lot. And everyone looked cool.

But as a parent, if you tried to dab, it was definitely NOT COOL. In fact, it was downright uncool and would have kids scampering to get away from their very uncool and embarrassing parents.

The interesting thing about dabbing is that, as a physical movement, it's neither cool nor uncool per se. It's an arbitrary movement that has no meaning other than the social meaning collectively attributed to the move by the social system around it – in this instance, young kids.

What makes it cool for one group (kids) and uncool for the other group (parents) is our social expectation of the behaviour of each group. We expect kids to dab, that's their role. When parents dab, they are now acting outside of their social expectation as a parent. Parents don't dab – that's not their role, it's just embarrassing. 'Like, oh my god, what are you doing? Just stop. You're embarrassing me.' Parents should act like parents, and kids should act like kids. That's what the kids think. So, when parents act like kids, the social system around them (the kids) gives them an 'electric shock' that kicks them back into their own roles (usually through some obvious eye rolling, back turning or walking away from their parents). The parents take the hint (if the kids are lucky!) and will revert to their 'normal' parent behaviour. Problem solved. Everyone is happy.

Social backlash works the same for women in the workplace.

> When women act in ways that are generally associated with male behaviours (often seen as strong leadership traits) rather than female ones (supportive and cooperative traits), they receive a negative backlash to get 'back in their box' or, in this case, back in the classroom.

Performance backlash

When women act within the expectations of their gender stereotype ('ladylike' over 'leaderlike'), they are fouled for being incompetent. Not because they are incompetent, but because they are being benchmarked against a different (and stubbornly pervasive) version of competence – the male model. When most leaders are men, it's hard to shake the unconscious link between male behaviours and successful leadership behaviours (despite the clearly established efficacy of women's leadership styles – refer to chapter 1). Women leading like women experience a performance backlash. Their value is less visible. They have to work harder to be seen as competent, because perception trumps performance.

Take the case of Sam. Sam was a highly experienced and competent executive-level leader who knew she wasn't taken seriously by upper management. In fact, her boss often told her she needed to act more like a 'leader' – tougher, stronger and more authoritative. She had made a concerted effort to work on this for six months and was doing really well. She was having hard conversations, giving tough feedback, pulling people up. She was really stepping up. Her performance had changed significantly; unfortunately, however, her manager disagreed. He didn't see these day-to-day actions. He wasn't looking for the changes created by her actions. She may have been holding people to account, but her style was still too soft for his liking. He was seeing what he expected, and his existing perception was confirmed during a meeting he attended with Sam. Another person in the meeting started behaving poorly. Sam's boss gave her an expectant look, nudging her to deal with the situation. She nodded in understanding.

After the meeting, Sam took the man aside, privately, and gave him the hard feedback. He was duly dealt with – only her boss didn't think so. He thought Sam was being weak and had caved in to the man. Why? Because she let the behaviour go in the moment and had the conversation privately, so as not to publicly shame him on his first warning (female conditioning to save face perhaps coming through). Her boss, on the other hand, expected her to reprimand him in front of the others (male conditioning to maintain status perhaps coming through). So even though in private Sam was very strong and direct with the man, it wasn't witnessed by her manager. Ergo, it didn't happen. And she hadn't changed. Not true, on both counts. Because the manager saw her behaviour through a skewed lens, however, his perception of her performance trumped the reality of her performance.

Perception also plays a role in job fit. Women are judged on how well they are *perceived* to fit into a role, rather than how much they actually do fit into a role. As an example of this, in 2005, researchers at Yale University put a group of subjects through a recruitment simulation. Their job was to hire the right candidate to fill the role of Police Chief. They were given two choices – a streetwise but well-liked police officer without much formal education, and a highly educated, polished official with little field experience; the classic book smarts versus street smarts. The participants were firstly asked to rate the two candidates by education versus street experience, and secondly to rate the importance of each criterion to the role itself. That is, is it more important for the Police Chief to have book smarts or street smarts?

Here's where it gets interesting. As outlined in the resulting research article, 'Constructed criteria: Redefining merit to justify discrimination', when people evaluated the resumes of the fake candidate called 'Michael', they amplified whatever factor he had the most of. So, when he was shown as having more street smarts, that's what got a higher importance rating; when he was shown as having more book smarts, that's what got the tick for being most important. These results didn't flow through for our fake female candidate 'Michelle', who received no such concessions, either way. The upshot was the people in the study thought the job would be better suited to a male candidate, and switched the required criteria accordingly. Perception trumps performance. (It is worth noting that the same shifting of weighted criteria happened against men when the role was a traditionally female role. Perception backlash affects both genders.)

Women and men at work

What's the role of perception? Consider the following:

- Women who have kids are viewed as less committed. Men who have kids are viewed as more responsible.[10]

- Women who have kids are assumed to be less competent and are therefore held to higher standards and presented with fewer opportunities.[11]

- Women are promoted on past performance. Men are promoted on future potential.[12]

- Women are twice as likely as men to be told they need to display 'more confidence'.[13]

- Women are one-third more likely than men to be told that they need 'more experience' to be ready for promotion, but only about 50 per cent of women are given the opportunity to gain the required experience.[14]

- Women are less likely than men to receive clear feedback on what they need to do to be ready for promotion.[15]

- Women are given feedback about their manner and communication style. Men are given feedback linked to business acumen and outcomes.[16]

- Women are more likely to be told they are aggressive, while men are told they are assertive. In a study of over 200 performance reviews, researchers found that when someone is told they're too aggressive, 76% of the time it's a woman being told.[17]

- Women negotiate for promotions and raises as often as men but face more pushback when they do.[18]

- Women have to be 250 per cent more productive during post-doctoral fellowships (for example, prolific in publishing journal articles) to be rated as equally competent to men.[19] (Having to work harder is not just a 'feeling'.)

In other words, perception has a direct role in setting up the gender penalties that are the topic of this book. Women are getting fouled on the field when they try to play by men's rules. The feeling that you have to work twice as hard and be three times as good just to get off the bench is clearly rooted in research – and not in your imagination. And while it can feel disheartening to know this, it's also liberating. It's not until we know what's going on that we can change what's going on. In coaching, we like to say, 'You can't change what you're not aware of'. And so it is here. Let this insight give you the clarity and wisdom to better understand the game at play and prepare your next move.

In this chapter, I've helped you confront some hard truths; if you lead like a man, you get backlash for not acting like a woman, but if you lead like a woman, you get backlash for not being competent. This is why women are getting fouled on the field when playing by the current rules, built by men and for men. So why on earth are we still playing this game? I explore that in the next chapter.

Chapter 4

Why are we still playing this old game?

If we are playing like women and getting benched, or playing like men and getting fouled, why on earth are we still playing this old game at all? It's madness. It clearly doesn't work for a lot of women (and some men, for that matter), and it's obvious that things need to change. So why aren't they changing? Or at least why aren't they changing faster?

In most Western societies, we baulk at the conditions and expectations from the past. Not that long ago, women were not allowed to work once they got married, or allowed to travel overseas without being accompanied by a man, or not allowed into certain university courses because that wasn't a woman's place. These laws and societal expectations were clear in their discrimination and obvious in their exclusion – and they've rightly been removed.

In the workforce of today, however, it's a different story. While the level of overt discrimination has reduced considerably compared to 100 years ago, we have seen the rise of a new type of discrimination. And this discrimination is not born out of blatant sexism, but rather a blinkered naivety about the subtle forces still exerting their pull on the conditions that create inequality. We are dealing with a new challenge. We are dealing with second-generation bias.

Second-generation bias

Second-generation bias is subtle and sometimes invisible, yet all too pervasive. It's the prejudice and inequality embedded in the fabric of our corporate lives that creeps into our cultures from a multitude of angles and attitudes, making the status quo hard to shake.

> **The systems, structures, policies and practices inherited from the past create barriers for women and boosters for men.**

It may not be overt or malicious, but it does exist. And it's not men against women; it's society's expectations of us all. And it's why women often find themselves on the sporting field in men's sporting gear, wondering why their big boots fly off every time they kick a goal. Everyone is on the field and everyone has the uniform, but the women's metaphorical uniforms just don't fit properly. They were never meant for women.

These 'uniforms' weren't necessarily created by the men currently playing on the field, but nevertheless the men on the field are still bolstered by the properly fitting attire, while women are blocked by it. This is why men don't feel they are being biased and why women may not feel explicitly or deliberately disadvantaged by today's men. And yet the game is still rigged. In fact, Professor Boris Groysberg of Harvard Business School demonstrated this point with his research on thousands of Wall Street analysts over many years. He found that the factors that led to an analyst's success at work differed for men and women. For men, their success was attributed to 40 per cent individual factors, 40 per cent company factors and 20 per cent luck. For women, it was closer to 80 per cent individual factors and 20 per cent luck, and nothing from the company. Men were bolstered by the corporate cultures they operated in, but women were not. They couldn't rely on the company to support their success.

Another example is out of this world … literally. In 2019, Anne McClain and Christina Koch, two NASA astronauts, were scheduled to take a spacewalk together on Friday, 29 March. This was to be an historic event – the first female-only spacewalk. However, on 25 March, McClain pulled the pin on her scheduled walk, thereby giving up her place in history. Why? It turns out they only had one 'space-ready' suit small enough to fit the two women. They did, however, have plenty of larger 'space-ready' suits to fit the men, so a man was swapped in at the last minute to take the place of Anne. History making would have to wait.

NASA suffered a great deal of backlash with this announcement, which prompted Anne McClain to jump to its defence and send a video message from space, claiming the decision was not due to sexism but rather a choice based on safety – her choice, more to the point. It seems the situation was not as clear-cut as some of the media reports made it out to be. Unfortunately, the fact remains that, for whatever reason, not enough space suits were available to accommodate two women to do a spacewalk in a medium-sized (better fitting and safer) suit at the same time. So one woman missed out. While it may not have been due to overt bias in the space station per se, as refuted by McClain, the systemic problem inherited from a time when all astronauts used to be men still exerts its influence on the careers of female astronauts today. No space suits, no space walks. End of story.

But it's not just in big moments such as this NASA example when we see the effects of second-generation bias. It's pervasive in our everyday work lives, even at the most ordinary levels. Charlene was a client of mine who worked for a manufacturing company. She said her company had only just started to focus on installing female toilets across the business a few years ago. Up until then, the women in the area had to walk five to ten minutes on to the plant site to get access to the nearest toilet. This wasn't because the men were gathered around secretly trying to sabotage the women, but simply because they had never had women on site before, so they didn't even realise there were no toilets for them.

And this issue doesn't just occur on the work site; it's also in our governments. In the ABC series *Ms Represented*, Annabel Crabb shares the history of inequality through the story of toilets in our governments with the arrival of Edith Cowan at the Parliament of Western Australia, in 1921. As the first female elected to an Australian parliament, Edith quickly learned that she may have had a seat at the table, but she would not get one in the loos. No female toilets were provided in the building and, to add insult to injury, they didn't install one for her either. Apparently, Edith's appointment was a 'freak occurrence' and unlikely to be repeated, so what was the point? For three years, Edith had to high tail it home to hit the loo in her own house.

The situation for women didn't improve in federal government either. In 1943, Enid Lyons and Dorothy Tangney were the first women to add their voices to the chorus of men, as the new members of federal parliament. And yet they too were left without a loo ... until 1974. Federal parliament had no female toilets until 1974! Women could run for our national parliament in 1902, but they weren't allowed to take a bathroom break in their own place of work for seven more decades. This is second generation bias. The systems and structures that hold women back and boost men up.

And if you think this is just a story from the 'past', think again. Women are still campaigning to this day. In 2015, women from the New South Wales parliament were campaigning to get the men's and women's gyms bathrooms swapped over – not rebuilt, just swapped over to better accommodate their needs. The building was built in the 1970s when only a handful of women were members of parliament, but of course it no longer served the 38 women there in 2015. The women discovered that the toilets in the men's gym had large mirrors, a half-circle of basins, 30 lockers and a bunch of toilets, while the women's had only two basins, two toilets, a couple of mirrors and a small area with eight lockers. Oh, and each level of Parliament House offered three men's showers and only one women's shower. Second-generation bias is obviously not just about the lack of toilets for women. However, when second-generation bias is reviewed through the lens of the ladies' loos, it paints a compelling picture of the plight of women.

The role of men

Second-generation bias is entrenched in our game of work, not just because of its hold on our systems and structures, but also because men don't feel the effects of it and are, therefore, less motivated to change it. Men don't realise their work site is missing female toilets because they don't use them. Men don't realise no small space suits are available because they don't wear them. Men don't realise they wouldn't make it onto the short list for an interview if they were a woman, even with the skills and experience required, because they are a man – ergo, they're on the shortlist.

This is not about a belief in gender equality; it's about the actions taken (or not taken) to prevent their impacts. It's hard to take action toward changing a system when that system doesn't negatively affect you. Interestingly, McKinsey & Company's study *Women in the Workplace 2015* found the following:

> *There appears to be a disconnect between men's interest in gender diversity and their understanding of the challenges women face: 70 per cent think gender diversity is important, but only 12 per cent believe women have fewer opportunities.*

Men believe in the ideals of gender equality but aren't grasping the realities of that inequality. And, yes, it's not all men. I know many passionate male allies and advocates are fighting for equality too – but not enough of them. We are still playing this game, because it still suits the majority who play it. Whether men believe in gender equality or not, it's an effort to change something that fundamentally favours you. And that holds true for all genders.

We are still playing this old game because women just weren't in the conversation when the game began.

> The decisions, the structures, the policies and procedures, the codes, the rules, the unwritten expectations, handed down through the generations, remain largely unexamined and unchallenged – especially by men. Men don't experience the biases that women experience. This is what causes our systems to remain stuck in size 'large' when a lot of us need a 'small'.

Over the last four chapters we've explored the state of play to better understand the game we've inherited. And what a doozy it is – old rules, ill-fitting equipment, perpetuating stereotypes, intractable structures and confusing penalties. We clearly have room for improvement when it comes to including women in the game of work. And rather than wait for the system to change itself, we must do what we can to start making an impact in the moment. Women bring amazing skills, talents and perspectives. The game of work clearly needs our input. It's time to bring our voices to the club room.

In the chapters in the next part, we start our foray into the gender penalties – what they are, what they mean and how you can work around them to make your mark on the game. Let's begin.

Notes

PART II

THE GENDER PENALTIES

penalty

/ˈpɛn(ə)lti/

noun

1. a punishment imposed for breaking a law, rule, or contract.
2. (in sports and games) a handicap imposed on a player or team for infringement of rules.

Welcome to the gender penalties that sideline women from the main game of work. Over the next few chapters, I unpack the obstacles women face and outline how to overcome them. And, no, this is not about giving up the fight to fix the system and focusing on fixing ourselves instead. This is about adapting our behaviours in the moment, so we can stay on the field and advance the game in the long term.

I've broken each chapter into the following sections to provide a clear playbook:

· **The penalty:** The invisible obstacle women face that sidelines them from the main game.

· **The current play:** What the research tells us is happening for women at work facing this penalty.

· **The rules:** A summary of the rules that work for men but don't work for women.

· **The backlash:** A figure outlining the negative feedback that results from following rules (meant for men, not women). The two types of backlash are external backlash, which comes from other people, society, culture, policies and so on, and internal backlash, which comes from ourselves. (Yes, that's right, we've become so conditioned to behave in certain ways that we start to criticise and condemn our own behaviour. Who needs enemies when we have our faithful inner critic?!

- **The stories from the field:** The experiences from other women who have faced the penalty – you are not alone!

- **Adapting the play:** The strategies and solutions that help women navigate the penalty and stay on the field.

- **The playbook summary:** A summarised checklist of the strategies and solutions to help you adapt your play. It includes Pre-game attitudes and On-field actions.

- **The personalised playbook:** A place to record your ideas and commitments to yourself.

As a bonus, I've also created *the coaches play* – a digital resource to share with your manager. It provides practical advice for leaders and managers to support women navigating the gender penalties in their role. This resource is a great way to help your boss, help you and shift the system at the same time.

I also invite you to take the quiz! If you want to know how you fare overall on the field against the gender penalties before we begin, take my Gender Penalty quiz. This quiz shows you where to focus your efforts to get the biggest bang for your buck from each of the strategy plays. You can also take the quiz again once you've finished reading the book, to see how far you've come.

To grab the coaches' play resources and fill in the Gender Penalty quiz, go to www.thegenderpenalty.com/bonuses.

Chapter 5

Penalty #1: Confidence

Confidence is the belief and trust in one's ability to do well. It's an inner knowing that motivates you into action. In the workplace, confidence is the critical launch pad for new skills, new opportunities and new jobs. It is the conviction that puts your perspective on the map and the drive that gets your wheels into motion. Confidence for women is a conundrum, however. Women are told to be more confident, but when they display more confidence, they are often seen as too arrogant. When they downplay their confidence, they become invisible. Men who display confidence, on the other hand, are seen as more competent. Simply telling women to 'be more confident', it seems, misses the point.

Current play

What's really going on with women and their confidence? How is women's relationship to their confidence different from men's, and how is this affecting their game at work? Why are women seen as less confident than men? What is the role of context and conditioning? How is the perception of confidence affecting their career opportunities? And what are the unwritten rules women are supposed to follow and the resulting backlash if they break them? In this section, I explore the current game being played with respect to confidence for women at work.

Women and men are born with equal confidence

That's right – overall, men and women start off with equal levels of confidence. Research has proven very few innate differences exist between men and women in terms of personality, cognitive ability, leadership and confidence.[20] We are not hardwired to doubt ourselves any more than men are hardwired to rate themselves. Men and women have mostly equal levels of confidence throughout their lives until they get to the workforce[21] (with a brief exception during puberty where the confidence levels of girls drop). But, despite equal ambition levels when entering the workforce, after about 10 years women's ambition levels start to drop.[22] And after about two to five years in the workplace, women start reporting lower rates of confidence.[23] Why?

Women lack confidence in the context, not their competence

In 2017 McKinsey & Company released their *Women Matter: Time to Accelerate* report, which summarised ten years of research into gender diversity. Their findings showed that women report lower levels of confidence at work but not due to their confidence in themselves, but to the confidence that they will be able to succeed in their work environment. The cultural messaging they get starts to wear them down, and they lose confidence in their ability to get ahead at work. Women experience more microaggressions than men – such as being talked over, being asked to explain or defend or justify, being more harshly penalised for mistakes or being mistaken for someone more junior. And when women respond confidently in job interviews, they are viewed as less likeable and not a good fit for the job.[24] All of these subtle signals about value reduce a woman's confidence in her ability to succeed in the workplace.

Women are not born less confident; they become less confident when the system doesn't support their confidence cues equally.

Women are conditioned to display less confidence

As discussed in chapter 2, professor of linguistics Dr Deborah Tannen has also highlighted how girls are socialised from an early age to downplay their certainty, whereas boys are taught to minimise their doubts. Modesty creates influence and confidence creates backlash. So even if they feel confident, women are often rewarded for downplaying that confidence in social settings, and particularly in the workplace. Women are not born less confident; they are conditioned to display less confidence.

Women are perceived as having low confidence

Because women are conditioned to display less confidence and penalised when they are overly (normally?) confident (read: arrogant), women are perceived as being less confident. In a 2017 report from Chief Executive Women, *Advancing Women in Australia: Eliminating Bias in Feedback and Promotions*, the authors highlighted that women are 2.5 times more likely than men to be told they need to be more confident. This also means that, as a result of constantly being told you're lacking confidence, you start to believe you have no confidence and your confidence drops even more, reinforcing the negative loop. Social psychologist Brenda Major from the University of California in Santa Barbara has studied self-perception of performance and confidence for decades. Her findings show that women tend to underestimate their ability and subsequent performance, and men tend to overestimate their ability and subsequent performance.[25]

Women are not given permission to be confident. Even if they are confident, they're likely to downplay it. And downplaying it can also create the perception of low confidence. And so, the cycle continues.

Women take less action

As a result of being conditioned to show less confidence and being penalised for being overly confident, women are more likely to wait too long before taking action, putting themselves forward or having a go. Women hold back while men push forward – and so men can be rewarded with jobs they've had no experience in, assignments that will stretch them and opportunities they might not even be ready for. Their confidence is perceived as capability and this creates a cycle of confidence that has men spinning upwards towards greater success and women spiralling downwards towards less success. As journalist Catherine Fox highlights in *Stop Fixing Women*:

> *Many commentators fail to acknowledge that the lack of confidence so loudly hailed as the culprit here is actually the result of the bias and discrimination woven into the attitudes and assumptions women face every day, year in and year out. Not the cause of it.*

Summarising the Confidence rules

'Be more confident.' 'Have a go.' 'Take a risk.' 'Back yourself.' 'Put yourself forward.' 'Get in the game!' 'Put your hand up.'

Backlash from the Confidence penalty

The figure overleaf highlights the Confidence rules and provides an example of the backlash in action. The external sources represent the backlash that comes from people around you (such as managers and colleagues) when you try to show confidence. The internal sources represent backlash that comes from your own thinking (based on your beliefs and perceptions) when you try to show confidence.

I've also provided further examples in the following bullets.

External:

- 'You're too arrogant.'
- 'Too self-assured.'
- 'Too cocky.'
- 'Tone it down.'
- 'You're too much for people.'
- 'You're not ready yet.'
- 'You need more experience.'

Internal:

- 'I'm not good enough.'
- 'I'm an imposter.'
- 'Who am I to do this?
- 'I don't feel ready.'
- 'I haven't had enough experience.'
- 'When will I be caught out?'
- 'They have more experience/more degrees/more connections/ more training ...'

Sits at the back of the room.

Doesn't go to important networking events.

Doesn't push for better roles and responsibilities.

Stories from the field

Nicole used to have a brilliant reputation. She smashed targets, brought in millions in revenue and knew her value to the business. However, over time she faced a number of challenges that began to erode her confidence. Eventually, she started to lose her edge

and people began to notice. By the time a new leadership role came up, her boss told her she was not on the list for promotion. 'You're just not confident. You're not senior leadership material,' she said. The little confidence Nicole had left crumbled, and she became crippled with self-doubt.

A few months after my masterclass, I received an email from Nicole. She sounded like a different woman with a different career. I could hardly believe what I was reading. She said her boss thought she was a totally different person, three months on from the program. She trusted Nicole, asked for her opinion and pulled her into important meetings – something she had never done before. But it wasn't just her boss who noticed the change; other partners from the leadership team were noticing her great work and congratulating her for her efforts, too. Finally, she had achieved her goal – she had reclaimed her brilliant reputation.

In light of such a drastic turnaround and to have earned such high praise, you would be forgiven for thinking that Nicole had become a much better operator. The truth was she performed to the same standard as before, but she did it with more confidence and conviction. She said,

> I am no more intelligent or groundbreaking than I was before, but my boss sees my work differently because of how I'm showing up. It's truly incredible. The key to my miraculous transformation is that I made the decision to be more confident. I really pushed myself. I was sick of not feeling valued and being told I 'wasn't ready'. I needed to prove people wrong. I wanted to impress them and deliver like I knew I could.

And so she did. The more actions she took, the more confidence she felt and the more traction she built. All of a sudden, her value was being recognised for what it had been all along.

Adapting the play for Confidence

Adapting the play is about changing your behaviour during the game – in this case, to overcome the Confidence penalty. This is not about pompoms and rah rahs and 'go get 'em' cheer squads. This is about understanding your own relationship to confidence and the impact that society's conditioning has had on how you choose to own it and display it. Whether you need to build actual confidence, build the perception of confidence, or stand against the backlash of 'too much' confidence, the following strategies will help you tackle the issue of confidence as a woman at work.

Confidence equals competence – take action

In the game of work, we equate confidence with competence. If someone presents with confidence, we naturally assume a higher level of competence. The reverse is also true – and whether they are actually competent or not is irrelevant.

If you wait for confidence to show up before you take action, you'll never get off the couch. The irony of confidence is that it acts like fitness. You have to exercise when you are unfit, in order to get fit. You don't sit at home waiting to become fitter before going to the gym (if only!). Confidence is the same. You have to do the very thing you are not confident about, in order to build your confidence. Once you get into action, you create a feedback loop of competency that demonstrates (to yourself and to others) that you can learn, you can grow and you are capable. So, let's get moving.

Be confident in your character – back your nous, not your knowledge

The quickest way to lose confidence is to compare yourself to someone who knows more, achieves more and handles more than you (or at least appears to). But if you think about it, they had to start somewhere. No accomplished person ever started with the full set of skills they currently have. They were (and still are) a perpetual work in progress – always building new skills. And so, the key to being as competent as the next person is to trust your ability to learn – back your nous, not your knowledge. You can learn anything if you put your mind to it. The key is to begin.

> Be confident in your character, not confident in your competence. With this as your guiding mindset, you will always be up for any challenge, whether you're 'ready for it' or not.

Accept the label – and be confident anyway

If you feel confident on the inside and show confidence on the outside, be okay with the label of 'arrogant'. If people see your healthy confidence as arrogance, that's on them. If you need them onside, you may 'tone it down' in the moment, but if this doesn't matter to you, then let them believe whatever they like. You know the truth. The people who really know you also know the truth. The more people see healthy confidence in women (and not just men), the more we normalise the behaviour for all confident women. In time, we can change this stereotype.

Challenge the value of over-confidence – don't become seduced

The most pervasive part of this problem is our over-investment in the value of confidence. It's the perception piece. From a systemic point of view, you need to challenge the prevailing stereotypes. You need to shift the conversation from building confident women to challenging overconfident men and dismantle the prejudice that punishes one and rewards the other.

In his book *Why Do So Many Incompetent Men Become Leaders? (And How to Fix It)*, author and academic Tomas Chamorro-Premuzic makes a case for the value of caution, humility and being careful –

that is, not being overly confident. He argues that men's character flaws (being overly confident sometimes to the point of arrogance) 'help them emerge as leaders because they are disguised as attractive leadership qualities'. He suggests that overconfidence can often signal bad leadership, and these behaviours are more common in the average man – hence, we end up with a system that rewards men for their incompetence and punishes women for their competence.

According to Chamorro-Premuzic, overconfidence is the result of privilege. Privilege is the result of unchallenged stereotypes. To break the cycle, we must challenge the stereotype. The next time someone appears overly confident (and simultaneously persuasive) be sure to challenge their stance – especially if you have counter-information based on facts. Don't be swayed by their confidence; be curious about the basis of it. Ask for more information. Ask for evidence. Get them to back it up with concrete data, not just confident prose. Let's neutralise the seductive quality of confidence and bring it back to facts. And don't let their confidence shake yours.

Value low confidence – know when it's caution

Low confidence and caution both appear as hesitancy, but they are not the same. One is based on a lack of self-belief and the other on a need to take care before moving forward. In pursuit of improving the perception of confidence, we must not give up our intuitive response to risk.

Make sure you understand the difference between when you're feeling low confidence due to conditioning and when you're feeling low confidence due to caution, concern or some instinct that tells you to be more careful. The distinction is critical and you must take care not to ignore your caution in favour of appearing confident. Signpost the difference, and don't squash your instinct.

Playbook summary

The following is a summary of the attitudes and actions to help you adapt your play when you hit the Confidence penalty. To create your own personalised playbook, put a tick next to the strategies that resonate with you.

Pre-game attitude

☐ Be confident in your character – be willing to learn.

☐ Decide to be more confident.

☐ Change 'not confident', to 'not confident "yet"'.

☐ Remember all the times you were confident to remind yourself you can do it.

☐ Draw on times you thought you couldn't but you did.

☐ Remember that everything you are good at now, you practised over time, so give yourself time.

☐ Brave the backlash of being perceived as 'too confident' over the risk of being 'invisible'.

☐ Keep in mind you can't get good until you get going.

☐ Recall a colleague who has been promoted over you because you weren't seen as confident enough (read: capable) even though you were more skilled. Do you want to work for people less capable than you? Didn't think so. So let's get moving. ☺

☐ Know the difference between confidence and caution – honour your instincts.

On-field action

☐ Do more things that scare you.

☐ Say yes to new things.

☐ Move when you are 40 per cent ready.

☐ Volunteer for things you will learn from.

☐ Celebrate failure as progress over perfection.

☐ Create a courage experiment to get outside your comfort zone.

☐ Make friends with incompetence by purposefully doing something you're 'not good at' (and notice you can still choose to feel confident even if you're not yet competent).

☐ Stop telling other women to be more confident. Instead, give them stretch opportunities to actually build their confidence and give them lots of encouragement and positive reinforcement.

☐ Challenge the confident knowledge of others. Push for evidence, data and facts and don't be swayed by delivery.

Mantra:
Move before I'm ready with confidence in my character.

Remember:
You can choose confidence; this is not about building it, it's about reclaiming it. You are ready right now. Go for it!

Bonus:
If you want your manager to know how to support you in the game, download the Coaches' Playbook for this penalty at www.thegenderpenalty.com/bonuses.

Personalised playbook for the Confidence penalty

What stood out to you from this chapter? What will you do differently as a result?

Use the following personalised playbook to record your ideas and commitments to yourself.

Insights

What resonated most with you from this chapter?

_____

_____

_____

Actions

What three actions will you take or do differently going forward? (With whom, in what context, by when?)

1. _____

_____

2. _____

_____

3. _____

_____

_____

Chapter 6

Penalty #2: Communication

Communication is a critical workplace skill. As a leader, your voice is your value – including how you use it, when you use it and how it's heard. It is a way to contribute value, demonstrate knowledge, influence outcomes, build relationships and build your leadership brand – unless you're a woman. Then it's not so straightforward. When men speak up, their voices are valued. When women speak up, their contributions are often challenged. This makes being seen and heard a constant battle for women in the workplace.

Current play

Why are women's voices overlooked and undervalued? Why does society hear women differently when they speak and what can we do about it? In this section, I explore the current game being played with respect to how men and women communicate at work. This is not just about getting women to speak up more; it's about getting society to listen more.

Women are silenced

Contrary to the common perception that women talk more than men in the corporate setting, the reverse is true. Study after study shows that in the workplace (and in other settings, including classrooms, courtrooms, media and politics) women are routinely interrupted, talked over, ignored and overlooked – or have their ideas claimed by others. In mixed groups, women speak less than men. This isn't because they don't have anything of value to say, however; it's because they can't get a word in edgeways. Men are given more space to talk and take up more space when they talk. Remember the conditioned communication expectation for men (as discussed in chapter 2) is about power and dominance – they take up more space. For women it's about cooperation and connection – they allow others more space. This dynamic, especially in a meeting context, means men are likely to speak up and women are likely to be shut down. And this has been reinforced by society almost since both sexes began talking.

Here are some fun facts for you (read: not fun at all):

· Men dominate meeting conversations about 75 per cent of the time.[26]

· Men interrupt women three times more than they interrupt other men.[27]

· Women interrupt others to add to the current conversation, while men interrupt others to redirect to a new conversation.[28]

· When women are outnumbered, they speak for between a quarter and a third less time than the men.[29]

· Male doctors will interrupt their patients, especially if they are women, but patients don't interrupt or talk over their doctors unless the doctor is a woman.[30]

· In 2016, Google's speech-recognition software was found to be 70 per cent more likely to accurately recognise male speech.[31]

· Women need to constitute a super majority of 70 per cent of a room in order to achieve parity and influence.[32] If they don't reach this percentage, they have difficulty being perceived as powerful, influential or important speakers.

- When women speak 30 per cent of the time in mixed-gender conversations, listeners think they dominate.[33]

- Boys speak nine to ten times more than girls in classrooms.[34]

- Parents interrupt their girls at almost twice the rate of boys.[35]

- In Western classrooms, boys are allowed by adults to consume five times as much verbal space as girls.[36]

- A study of Harvard undergraduate classrooms found that male students speak at least three times more than female ones.[37]

Women are undervalued

In her compelling book *Rage Becomes Her: The Power of Women's Anger*, author Soraya Chemaly references studies that show women are 'more likely to be doubted when we speak in the workplace, in courts, in politics, in situations involving the police, and in medical consultations with doctors and hospital staff'. Women's ideas are discounted and their competency is assumed to be lacking compared to men (often by both sexes, because: unconscious stereotypes). Women have to work harder to be seen as competent, regardless of their ability to communicate with authority.[38]

Consider the following:

- When offering software change recommendations in the open-source software community, women's suggestions are accepted more often than men's, unless their gender is identifiable ... then they are rejected more often.[39]

- Senior men in Australian business are twice as likely to rank other men over women as effective problem-solvers, despite believing that women are as capable as men in delivering outcomes.[40]

- Switching to blind auditions for orchestra recruitment (using screens to hide gender) is responsible for between 30 and 55 per cent of the increase in the proportion of new recruits being female.[41]

- One study found, replacing a woman's name with a man's on a résumé increases their odds of being hired by 71 per cent.[42]

- During post-doctoral fellowships, women have to be a whopping 250 per cent more productive to be rated as equally competent to men[43] (see chapter 3).

> As a society, we assume men are competent – while we make women prove their competence. This means women are asked to defend, justify, prove or explain their ideas more than men are.

A collective hangover from centuries of stereotypical conditioning means women's contributions and competencies are discounted. They are filtered through the gender lens and taxed because of our sex. Women are not believed.

Case in point: as part of writing this book, I bought a lot of books for research purposes. (Okay, that's an excuse ... I always buy a lot of books, but I digress ...) One day I was signing for delivery of yet another book, when the postie remarked, 'You like to read?'

'Yes.' I replied. 'But I'm writing a book so it's mostly for research.'

'What are you writing about?' he asked.

'Business', I replied.

To which he responded, 'Oh. I don't mean to be rude, but what do you know about business?'

I stared at him blankly. 'A lot actually. I've been running my own business for over 15 years. But it's not about how to run a business. It's about women in leadership.'

'Oh. Yes, we need more of them.'

Indeed, we do. Now, my postie wasn't being nasty or purposefully diminishing, but my instinct tells me that if he'd had that conversation with my husband, he would not have asked him what he knew about business. And yet, it is somehow socially acceptable to ask me to prove my capability. To just accept that I, as a woman, am qualified enough to write a book about business is a bridge too far. (Unless it's about women's things – then that's believable.)

A friend of mine shared an equally frustrating story on LinkedIn – on National Pay Equity Day. Sally Parrish is the founder and Director of the Board Coaching Institute. She works with some heavy hitters. She's as smart as a whip, has a long list of achievements and has a huge capacity to get things done. Yet she knows all too well how women are undervalued. I'll let her tell the story ...

> *I'm busy working on a new Members Area for my clients and Bill (the male expert that I've hired) and I have been plugging away for hours, for days, for weeks to get this system up and running.*
>
> *Last week we hit a roadblock. We couldn't get the system to perform an essential task we needed it to.*
>
> *Bill opened a support ticket and composed a short message along the lines of 'can't get system to do x – please advise the steps'.*
>
> *We received a long-winded reply about the merits of the system and a difficult explanation of how to do what we wanted to do that didn't quite seem to provide the fix we wanted.*
>
> *Bill replied, and laid out the problem again and explained why the solution wasn't the right fix.*
>
> *The Help desk replied again and said 'You don't understand' and again offered the fix that wouldn't work.*
>
> *Bill was really frustrated. 'They're usually much more helpful than this. I just need to know how to do x and then I can get on with it.'*

I explained to Bill that he was experiencing female bias/discrimination. He was inside my account, using my user details and they thought they were talking to a 'silly woman'.

Bill sent the same request, but with a small change to the message 'Hi. Bill here, helping Sally out with her system. She can't get system to do x – please advise the steps'.

What we received back was a simple step-by-step solution to fix our issue. It got us unstuck right away. They also added, 'If I can be of any further help or assistance, just reach out...'

Female asks for help = 'You don't understand'. Presupposes the woman doesn't have the ability to solve the problem.

Male asks for help = simple easy to follow advice and a 'reach out if I can be of any further help or assistance'.

Stop underestimating us.

To add insult to injury, when women do offer up great ideas, they are often claimed by others. I can't tell you how many times I've had women in my programs complain of an idea they've put forward being ignored, only to have it miraculously approved and applauded when a man, two or three suggestions later, offers it up again as his own.

An accomplished colleague of mine who has been on distinguished boards across the globe for many years (mostly as the only female) recently encountered one of the most inexcusable/gobsmacking examples of discounting and claiming credit that I have heard in a long time (and I have heard some doozies in my line of work!). Her board was having their monthly meeting and she made a suggestion about what to focus on in the coming year – being focused, brief and strategic. Three short points; succinct, clear, unequivocal.

The very next suggestion that came out of the next person to speak was her exact idea, in her exact words, but with one difference ... the man added, 'I'd like to propose a motion that next year we focus on being focused, brief and strategic'. Not as a way to restate her idea, give her a nod of acknowledgment, and boost her idea by formally sanctioning it. He restated her idea as if it were his own. She gave him a quizzical look, waiting for the attribution or acknowledgement of her idea, but none came. Puzzled and annoyed, she looked around the room. No-one said anything. Then, to add insult to injury, the other board members offered up the 'seconding' and 'thirding' required for the motion to be passed and formally recorded in the minutes as his suggestion ... for eternity. Perhaps feeling like she was in a cartoon similar to the one I've included here, my colleague was so shocked by the bad behaviour that she let it go in the meeting. Later that day, she called the Director concerned and gave him direct feedback regarding his unprofessional behaviour. He sheepishly confessed he hadn't even noticed that he had done it. She stressed that it should never happen again, or she would raise it in the meeting for minuting and also ask for a formal three-way discussion with the Chairman. It never happened again.

"That's an excellent suggestion, Miss Triggs. Perhaps one of the men here would like to make it."

Women are overlooked

Not only are women silenced in their speech and discounted in their contributions, they are accused of not 'sounding like a leader'. The typical voice of leadership as we know it is low, slow and deep. It is strong and direct and commanding in nature. (Think James Earl Jones in *Star Wars* ... 'Luke. I am your father.') These attributes are more closely aligned with male speech patterns than female ones. As highlighted in the *Forbes* article 'Women's ideas: Do men intentionally steal them?' by lawyer and author Caroline Turner, men's conditioned speech is typically stronger and more direct, whereas women's conditioned speech is more indirect and tentative, often peppered with apologies, disclaimers, tag questions and hedging language. (Again, this is not every woman, nor every man; however, these are the conditioned patterns we expect and, therefore, often encounter.) As a result, unconsciously, the voice of authority is the voice of a man.

> When women communicate, their voices, styles and speech patterns are unconsciously compared to the male model – and often come up lacking in credibility and authority.

In performance reviews, women are given twice as much feedback on their communication style as men.[44] Incidentally, men are given more feedback on their business acumen and technical skills (read: how to sound like a leader versus how to be a leader). This makes it easier to overlook the leadership capability of women and grossly undervalue their potential. If you don't communicate with authority, you mustn't have any authority, right? Sigh.

Belinda is an example of this. She was a sales manager on the rise, and was ambitious, accomplished and ready for her next move. She was also small in stature, affable with a ready smile, and looked (and sounded) younger than her years (lucky her!). She was introduced to a very senior man in her industry and, after a promising conversation, he agreed to be her sponsor. He could see her potential – for the most part. He said he would keep his eye open for any roles that came along that might suit her. It turns out he was sitting on a role he knew about, but didn't associate it with her level until they continued their communication via text. Here's how the text exchange went later in the day.

Him: 'Great to meet with you too. As promised, I'll keep my ear to the ground if anything comes up. Just for my clarification, do you prefer a sales role or a marketing role?'

Her: 'Ideally, I'd see a Head of Sales role as being my next step with opportunity to progress to General Manager – Sales and Marketing.' *[Her comment to me was, 'I would never normally be so direct about asking for what I want. I would normally say something like, "I've mostly worked in sales so I suppose I'd be looking for something in that space. But I'd also be happy with a role in marketing if you think I have enough experience. I'd just be grateful for the opportunity", but after the course I knew I had to explicitly ask for what I wanted.']*

Him: 'Okay, leave it with me.'

[Later on that day.]

Him: 'Are you okay with me giving your details to [bigwig] from [bigwig company]? He has a big job going right now. I didn't mention this earlier when we met because I thought it might be too senior but I have changed my mind after reading your message.'

He had seen her potential but not her time frames. She had to spell it out for him.

Recently, Belinda told me that that moment changed the trajectory of her career. It was a sliding doors moment that led to bigger and better opportunities, at an accelerated pace. She'd put herself on the map and went on to land a sales director role, shortly after. Yay her!

Summarising the Communication rules

'Speak up.' 'Be heard.' 'Have an opinion.' 'Have more executive presence.' 'Speak like a leader.' 'Be more credible.' 'Contribute more.'

Backlash from the Communication penalty

The figure overleaf highlights the Communication rules and provides an example of the backlash in action. The external sources represent the backlash that comes from people around you (such as managers and colleagues) when you try to speak up. The internal sources represent backlash that comes from our own thinking (based on your beliefs and perceptions) when you try to speak up.

I've also provided further examples in the following bullets.

External:

- 'What does your boss think?'
- 'How do you know that?'
- 'Are you sure about that?'
- 'I don't believe that.'
- 'I'm not sure you're ready yet.'
- 'You need to have more "presence".'
- 'You're not leadership material.'
- 'You need to contribute more in meetings.'

Internal:

- 'I don't want to talk over them.'
- 'I'm not 100 per cent sure about this idea.'
- 'All the good points have been made already.'
- 'I'm waiting for a break in the conversation.'
- 'I don't want to say something just for the sake of hearing my own voice.'

- 'My boss is here so they'll probably talk to my points now.'
- 'I feel intimidated when all eyes are on me so I don't articulate myself well.'
- 'He seems so confident so maybe he's right? Maybe I'm missing something?'
- 'They don't listen to me anyway so there's no point correcting them.'
- 'I just said that. Why aren't they listening to me?'
- 'That was my idea. Why didn't I get the credit? I can't call them out without looking like a b!%$#.'

Interrupted.

Cut off.

Ignored.

Talked over.

Discounted.

Not believed.

Questioned.

Mistaken for someone more junior, less qualified or less experienced.

Stories from the field

Kiera sat in the annual meeting. Every year, her team had to meet with the auditors to go over the books. Every year, they were questioned and scrutinised and their work was challenged. This particular year, Kiera listened as the conversation turned to a recurring problem. The group was going around in circles trying to understand and solve this problem.

Kiera could see the issue immediately but didn't say anything. The meeting was filled with people more senior than her and more confident-sounding than her. She wondered why no-one was mentioning the real issue. With so many loud, confident voices,

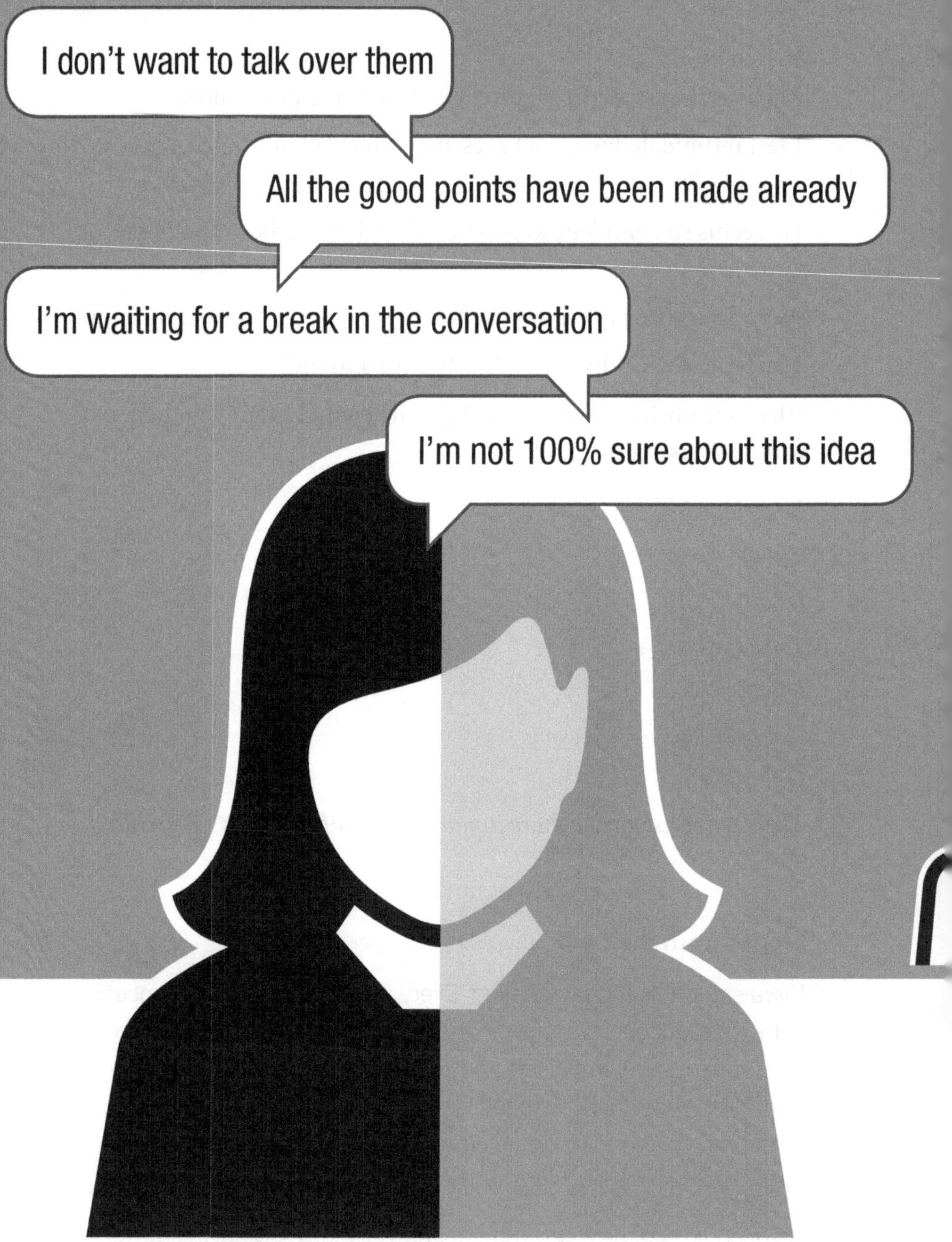

Internal Backlash
from ourselves

she wondered what they knew that she didn't know that made them not mention the obvious solution. It made her doubt what she knew and the value in speaking up.

Eventually, she bit the bullet and offered up her opinion. To her astonishment, it was met with head-slapping relief and gratitude. How stupid of them to completely miss that, they cried. It saved the company a bucket of money and it taught her a valuable lesson: just speak up. What have you got to lose?

Adapting the play for Communication

Adapting the play is about changing your behaviour during the game – this time to overcome the Communication penalty. As frustrating as it is to be the one who has to change their style in order to be heard, the harsh reality is if no-one gives you room to speak, you have to create it for yourself. Whether you need strategies to cut through or strategies to hold the floor, the following ideas will help you tackle the issue of communication at work.

Speak early, speak often – add your voice

The most common place to showcase your value is in a meeting. It's where you show people who you are, what you know and how you operate – but only if you speak up. When you pick up a phone call, you say something similar to, 'Hello, this is Anneli. How can I help you?' (Obviously, you don't use my name, but you get the drift.) You announce yourself on the call. You don't pick up the call and remain silent, leaving the other person wondering if you're there or not. Same goes for a meeting. If you're in the meeting, be in the meeting. Speak early so people know you're there and ready to contribute. Speak every 10 to 15 minutes so people know you are still there and still ready to contribute. And speak close to the end so people know you were there and you did contribute.

At this point, you might be thinking, *What if I don't have anything to say?*, *What if I'm new to the role?* or *I don't want to speak just for the sake of it*. And you don't have to speak just for the sake of it. But you do have something to say. You are observant, you are experienced at work and you have a perspective, even if you are new. In fact, especially if you are new.

> **You will have questions, observations and fresh insights. Use your perspective, past experiences and curiosity to make contributions. Or simply make statements to affirm the group and how you are communicating.**

Here are some examples:

- 'It's great to meet you all. I'm looking forward to working on this project.'
- 'I'm really glad that we're tackling this topic today. It's not an easy one, but it's the right thing for the customer.'
- 'I've noticed we've been talking about this topic for a while now. What do we need to make a decision at this point?'
- 'We haven't heard from Josie yet. What are your thoughts, Josie?'
- 'It sounds like Armin and Tei are saying the same thing, so what's the next step from here?'
- 'That's an important point, John. It mirrors my own experience from my last job. Happy to share more about that incident, too.'

Stop interruptions – teach respect

As social creatures, most women are hardwired to protect relationships. When people interrupt us, talk over us or ignore us, calling them on it can feel challenging. But call them on it, we must. This is not about bruising relationships; this is about building respect and redefining communication standards. Check out your digital bonuses for a great example of this in action (www.thegenderpenalty.com/bonuses). Find strategies you are comfortable with, to build confidence in using them.

Here are some examples:

- 'I'm not finished yet, Bob.'

- 'Let me finish, please. This is important.'

- 'Chris, would you mind not interrupting me? I want to finish my point here.'

- 'Angelica, what were you saying? You didn't get a chance to finish your thought before the conversation moved on. I'd like to hear it.'

- 'As I was saying ...'

Claim back credit – keep your ideas

When people restate your ideas and fail to pass the credit onto you, it can be frustrating to say the least. The temptation to express your anger and disappointment can be strong, but it's rarely productive as a first step. First, you need to give people the benefit of the doubt and assume it wasn't intentional. Address the behaviours in the moment and start training others to notice their behaviours. If a more direct approach is needed, you can use a stronger intervention in the moment and then address the issue offline as well.

You can use the following strategies (which offer varying degrees of directness) to reclaim credit and stop idea-theft from happening:

- 'Thanks for restating my idea, Sam. I'm glad you agree. The reason it's so important is because ...' (Add more to your idea to reinforce how much thinking you've done on it.)

- 'Thanks for your agreement on this. It's great to have your support. As I was saying ...'

- 'Thanks for rephrasing it like that. That's exactly what I meant when I said it. I'm glad you're on board too.'

- 'I just said that. Did you want to add something new or you just wanted to back up my point? I'm glad to have your support on this.'

- 'I just said that a minute ago. I feel like I'm not being heard in this meeting.'

- 'That's the second time you've restated my idea without giving me credit. I'm not sure if you're aware that you're doing it, but it's getting quite frustrating.'

- 'Please stop restating my ideas as your own. It's unprofessional.'

One of my clients, Jess, was one of two female managers in her team at a large retailer. She was talented, experienced and confident. A manager in her team constantly restated her (and others') ideas as his own. After a few months of group coaching with other women, sharing stories and swapping strategies, she decided enough was enough. One day in a meeting when he had once again stolen her idea, she came straight out and said, 'Hey. I literally just said that. Stop stealing my ideas. It's not cool.'

Tentatively others joined in. 'Ahh, actually, mate, you do that to me too.' 'Yeah, same here. It's kind of frustrating.' He was taken aback. He'd never had this feedback before. Eventually, he apologised to her and was much more careful in future meetings. It's important to note here that he wasn't stealing ideas on purpose, and nor was he targeting her. It was a behaviour that no-one had called him on before, so it went unchecked. We need to give the feedback and highlight the habit if we want to see change.

Speak like you mean it – be authoritative

In the workplace, your communication style is your currency for creating authority and impact. It buys you the right to be heard. If your communication isn't cutting through, and the system around you isn't doing its part to bring you into the conversation yet, then you need a new strategy. This isn't about speaking like a man; it's about speaking in a way that people can hear you better. It's a momentary shift to get attention and be taken seriously. And it's mostly about unconscious confidence cues.

Speaking with authority requires a delicate combination of vocal, verbal and non-verbal cues, but most people just need a few foundational principles to get them going. To catapult your communication credibility, focus on some of these strategies:

- Use short and simple sentences – fewer words equals greater impact.

- Drop the upward inflection – think 'serious parent voice' and dump the questioning tonality by lowering your tone at the end of your sentences.

- Expand your body posture – take up space, and don't minimise your presence.

- Take a stand, don't hedge your bets – be decisive in your opinion and don't downplay your authority with tentative, hedging language.

- Stop apologising as a habit of connection – save them for when you need them.

- Don't ask for permission to speak or ask a question – just speak.

- Dump the disclaimers that downplay your expertise – for example, 'I don't know much about this, but …', 'I'm not good with numbers, but …'.

- Stand up straight and steady – don't rock or shift your weight back and forth.

If you want more strategies in this area, you can download my cheat sheet of credibility killers and creators at www.thegenderpenalty.com/bonuses.

Playbook summary

The following is a summary of the attitudes and actions to help you adapt your play when you hit the Communication penalty. To create your own personalised playbook, put a tick next to the strategies that resonate with you.

Pre-game attitude

☐ Just because other people speak more often and with more confidence, this doesn't make their ideas any better than yours.

☐ Take a light approach to pointing out interruptions – humour and levity go a long way to diffusing tense moments.

☐ Give men (and other women) the benefit of the doubt when dealing with unhelpful behaviours.

☐ Remember this is not necessarily about you – it's a collective pattern – but you can still break the cycle.

☐ The more you speak up, the more you normalise women's voices and become a role model for other women.

On-field action

☐ Speak early and often in a meeting – no voice = no visibility.

☐ Speak in your lower register.

☐ Dump the questioning tonality and drop your tone at the end of sentences.

☐ Stand for something – don't hedge your bets.

☐ Don't let people interrupt you.

☐ Stand up straight and tall and expand in to the space – you deserve to be there.

Mantra: Your voice is your value. Use it or lose it.

Remember: Your voice is valid. You deserve to be heard as much as anyone else. Use your voice to make an impact. If they can't hear you, they can't heed you – so get into the conversation.

Bonus: If you want your manager to know how to support you in the game, download the Coaches' Playbook for this penalty at www.thegenderpenalty.com/bonuses.

Personalised playbook for the Communication penalty

What stood out to you from this chapter? What will you do differently as a result?

Use the following personalised playbook to record your ideas and commitments to yourself.

Insights

What resonated most with you from this chapter?

_____

_____

_____

Actions

What three actions will you take or do differently going forward? (With whom, in what context, by when?)

1. _____

_____

2. _____

_____

3. _____

_____

_____

Chapter 7

Penalty #3: Boasting

Getting ahead in your career is as much about visibility as it is about value. When everyone is expected to be a high performer, getting noticed is less about *doing* a great job and more about being *seen* to be doing a great job. Those who can showcase their work, spotlight their wins and highlight their achievements create a professional edge. They stay top of mind and first in line when opportunities are being offered. Society's distaste for women who boast, however, makes self-promotion a pain point for women. Men who talk up their professional achievements are seen as accomplished, whereas women who do the same are seen as boastful.

Current play

No-one likes a show-off, but in the world of work, we particularly despise these behaviours from women. But when women talk about their accomplishments are they really showing off or is that just how we hear it? Why does society support men to brag but abhor the same behaviour in women? And what happens to women's prospects when they stay humble and modest? In this section, I explore the current game being played with respect to how men and women are encouraged (or not) to showcase their abilities and highlight their strengths.

Men display, women downplay

As discussed in chapter 2, men have been conditioned to be competitive, to highlight their strengths and display their value, in order to win the game of work. Women, on the other hand, have been conditioned to be more communal, downplay their achievements and not elevate themselves above others. We have no problem with men talking themselves up or showcasing their achievements. Okay, we may not love it, but we don't punish them for it. We are used to hearing men make bold claims about their abilities and their achievements, and why they are right for the job, role or opportunity. Women, on the other hand, are mostly expected to act with modesty and humility, and not be too boastful. Added to this is the common refrain I hear from women – that their good work should speak for itself. It doesn't. It whispers into the whirlwind of loud voices, also doing good work *and* showcasing it.

Most women hate to brag or toot their own horn, so they have no problem with this societal expectation of women to downplay, diminish and discount. It's often automatic. Think about it. What happened the last time you complimented a woman? Did she say 'Thank you', full stop? Or did she discount, diminish or defer the compliment in some way? 'Oh, this old thing. I've had it for years. It's not that special.' 'Thanks, but it wasn't just me, it was a team effort. I didn't really have much to do with it.' 'It wasn't anything, really. Anyone could have done it.' 'Me? What about *you*? You were amazing out there!' Now you may not get this kind of response from every woman you compliment, of course, but chances are it's the most common. It's conditioning, remember. It also doesn't mean that anything is wrong with sharing the love around or not wanting to be in the spotlight; however, when it comes to the game of work, shifting the spotlight away from yourself and towards others (without being able to own your own part first) will play havoc with your personal brand and future potential.

Women are punished for self-promotion

Some studies have shown that women who act in self-promoting ways are considered undeserving, whereas men acting in the same way receive no such response.[45] Women who are seen to self-promote are deemed more unlikeable and (ironically) less likely to be promoted.[46] We also know that women are promoted at lower rates than men,[47] so we need all the visibility we can get. However, self-promotion creates a penalty for women and a push for men. Modesty is the antidote for many women. It enables influence and keeps the stereotypes in check – but it also keeps women playing small and flying under the radar.

Women stop claiming credit

As a result of our need to appease society through humility (and because it feels more comfortable), women stop claiming credit when it's offered.[48] Instead, they share credit with others. This means when it comes to claiming the credit, women step back and men step forward. And when women stop claiming credit, they stop getting credit. And down the spiral we go.

This is not to say that sharing credit is not a good thing to do. It is. In general. *But* if you constantly push credit away from yourself, you are signalling to people that you are not worthy. Plus, you are not allowing others to celebrate you. In the world of keynote speaking, we call that 'walking through the applause'. You're taught early on that professional speakers never walk through the applause. You must allow your audience to show their appreciation for you and accept it with grace and gratitude. As women, we have to stop 'walking through the applause'.

Summarising the Boasting rules

'Be more visible.' 'Advertise your achievements.' 'Share your strengths.' 'Be proud of yourself.' 'Celebrate your wins.' 'Take credit for your work.' 'Accept the compliment.' 'Let people know what you're good at.' 'Stop apologising.' 'To get the job/raise/promotion, you need to tell them why you deserve it.'

Backlash from the Boasting penalty

The figure overleaf highlights the Boasting rules and provides an example of the backlash in action. The external sources represent the backlash that comes from people around you (such as managers and colleagues) when you try to highlight your achievements. The internal sources represent backlash that comes from your own thinking (based on your beliefs and perceptions) when you try to highlight your achievements.

I've also provided further examples in the following bullets.

External:

- 'It's not ladylike to brag.'
- 'You need to be more humble.'
- 'You don't want to look full of yourself.'
- 'Don't be overly ambitious.'
- 'You're putting people off.'
- 'It's not all about you.'

Internal:

- 'I hate bragging.'
- 'I feel uncomfortable talking about myself.'
- 'My good work should speak for itself.'
- 'I don't want to appear full of myself.'
- 'I'm not one to boast or toot my own horn.'
- 'I hate being in the spotlight.'
- 'If my work is good enough, I shouldn't have to tell people about it.'
- 'It's not about me, it's about the team.'

Stories from the field

'That was a brilliant session, Anneli. I could see the team got a lot of value from the day and we're on track to getting this launch off the ground. Great work today, thank you. I'm curious about one thing – what was with that intro in the morning?'

'What do you mean? What did I do in the intro?'

'It's more about what you didn't do. You didn't introduce yourself properly. You didn't talk about who you had worked with or what you've achieved. You didn't mention you're an author, a speaker, an expert in your field. You didn't mention any of the big international brands you've worked with or what you've helped them achieve or any of your awards. You did a line or two about what you specialise in but that was it. You didn't even mention your new book! You had the heads of each business across Australia, with reporting lines internationally, sitting as a captive audience and you didn't position yourself as the authority up front. Why not?'

Yikes! I had been working with this CEO for many years. We had a good relationship and have had many direct conversations in the past, but this was one I was not expecting. I was taken aback. Not just because my introduction had not made the impression I had hoped but because of why I chose to skip my usual, more lengthy intro that would cover these items. I figured that I was known enough to this group that I didn't have to speak to my accomplishments. I assumed they knew enough about me to be on board with the mission for the day. And, more importantly, I assumed my good work would speak for itself. And there it is – the boasting penalty at play, even now. I was focused on doing good work, while the CEO was focused on drawing attention to the fact that I do good work. I was focused on building rapport; the CEO was focused on building my status.

Until this moment, I didn't realise how deeply ingrained the humility habit was and what kind of impact that was having. By not

Boasting Rules
for players

- Be more visible
- Share your strengths
- Be proud of yourself
- Celebrate your wins
- Take credit for your work
- Stop apologising

Don't be overly ambitious

It's not all about you

You need to be more humble

It's not ladylike to brag

You're putting people off

External Backlash
to women

reminding the group who I was, what I had done and why I had the credibility to be at the front of the room, I had done myself a disservice. Sure, they still experienced my value and could still come to me for help if they wanted to, but I hadn't made it easy for them. I hadn't spelled out the various things I'd done or the ways I could help them outside of the agenda for the day. I didn't plant the seed to partner in their success beyond the day. I played small in the beginning, relying on my great work to speak for itself. This was a missed opportunity in a room full of executives who value the success successful people can bring.

Adapting the play for Boasting

Adapting the play is about changing your behaviour during the game – this time to overcome the Boasting penalty. With the humility habit so hardwired, starting to showcase your strengths can feel like a stretch. The key is to use the following strategies to find a way to talk about yourself that doesn't make you want to throw up in your mouth ... even a little bit.

Visibility equals value – build a brag book

The rules of the game require all players to make themselves visible to the coach. If the coach doesn't know your strengths, your experience and your wins, you won't get picked for the team.

This is not about boasting; it's about boosting. You need to boost your visibility to bolster your value and get off the bench.

A simple way to stay visible to your manager (and boost without boasting) is to keep a brag book. Call it whatever you like, it's a way to record your weekly wins, achievements and accomplishments and share them in your monthly one-on-ones (and summarise them for your annual performance review as well!). Tell your boss the brag book helps you remember what went well so you can provide a balanced approach to reviewing your work. As humans, we tend to focus on development gaps and we forget to celebrate what's working well. This book helps you do both. You could also mention that women are often penalised for 'bragging', so a brag book helps you break this stereotype and normalise the process of women sharing wins in a safe, respected way. ☺

This simple but powerful strategy helps your boss help you. As much as you might like to think bosses are across all the amazing things you do, the reality is this is unlikely. They are busy, stretched and stressed, and looking after a whole team as well as their own career. You need to do what you can to be easy to remember, favourably. Incidentally, this also makes it easier for them to bat for you in talent discussions – where each manager has to argue for the bonuses and promotions of the people in their team. The more they know about your achievements, the easier you are to bat for. Trust me: humility keeps you hidden in these forums. It's not enough that you do well. You need to be known for doing well. You need to be visible to be valued.

Successful by association – talk it up

Those who talk about successful outcomes or present great work on behalf of others unconsciously get credited with the work – not the actual credit, but the emotional credit. Yep. It's not rational, it's not fair, but it does happen. This means that if women are shying away from the spotlight or leaving others to speak about their wins and successes, those wins are getting credited to the people talking about them, not necessarily the people doing them.

People feel good about good news and so they feel good about the bearer of the news. This is success by association – creating emotional credit. It works in a similar way to the bearer of bad news – the reason we have the saying, 'Don't shoot the messenger'. We know that people have a tendency to conflate the message and the messenger and unconsciously link them together. When it comes to achievements, if you say them, you share them.

Take every opportunity to report good news – yours, others', the team's. Be the bearer of great news to boost your brand. This is a neat way to brag without bragging. It doesn't need to be about you to impact you. And if you want a pro tip? Talk up other people, not just projects. It has the same outcome (transference of all the good feels to you) but with the added benefit of spotlighting someone else who needs a boost. It's a win–win.

Your words become their thoughts – say what you mean

When it comes to messages, humans are easily programmed by exposure and repetition. When we hear the same message over and over again, it unconsciously seeps into our brain and takes hold in the recesses of our mind. Take, for instance, things your parents used to say over and over again. 'Money doesn't grow on trees.' 'Time to lean, time to clean.' Whatever it was for you, I'm sure you could recite the things your parents used to say, in your sleep. The same phenomenon occurs when we talk about ourselves in diminishing ways. The more you say things like, 'I'm not good with budgets', or 'I'm not good with new systems', or 'Presentations freak me out', the more those messages get stuck in the brains of the people around you. And they *believe* you! They become programmed, by you, to think of you in the way you are training them to. Then when it comes time to put you forward for something, your words become their thoughts. And they come back to bite you. 'Let's give this to Margaret.' 'Ahh, she's not good with budgets. Let's give it to Tom instead. He's always up for a challenge.' Eeeek! We are constantly conditioning the people around us to think of us in certain ways.

We nudge the narrative of our brand, for better or worse. Never ever diminish your skills in front of others. Only talk about yourself in ways you want to be talked about. 'Budgets? Sure. I'll give it a go. I love learning new things.' 'Presenting at the next town hall? Yep. I'll do it. I love stretching myself out of my comfort zone.' 'Reviewing this code? You can count on me. I love a good challenge.' Your words become their thoughts. Speak wisely.

Take the credit – claim and redirect

Sometimes we need to claim our work in order to get the credit. When your contribution is invisible but you know it's important to claim it, you can use the 'claim and redirect' strategy. Claim the credit and then redirect their attention to further amplify your impact and soften the act of claiming the credit. Compare these two statements to see this in action:

- **Claim the credit:** 'Your team did a great job on the report. Especially that compound formula. Well done.' In response, you could say, 'Thanks for that. Yes, the team did a great job and I'm glad you appreciated the compound formula. I worked on that piece.' (Sounds a bit braggy, right?)

- **Claim and redirect:** 'Your team did a great job on the report. Especially that compound formula. Well done.' You respond with, 'Thanks for that. Yes, the team did a great job and I'm glad you appreciated the compound formula. I was the one to work on that piece and it almost had me beat! It was really complex. I was so determined to work it out, though, that I just kept at it until it was done. I'm really thrilled with the outcome. Not only do we now have the formula for this report, but the other teams can use it going forward as well. I'm so proud of myself.' (Sounds exciting, right?)

The key here is to claim the credit and then redirect their attention to why that was beneficial, for you and for them. Genius.

The power of passion – enrol them with emotion

Occasionally at work, we achieve big things that are worth an honest to goodness brag. This is a step beyond merely claiming credit and a move into boldly showcasing your achievements. The key to sharing your wins and spotlighting your strengths is to fully feel the joy. Own your pride, your happiness, your excitement. Emotions are contagious and if you feel good about the achievement, others will feel good as well.

I learnt this lesson when I received an award and posted a video about it on LinkedIn. I didn't even bother with the standard humble brag intro of 'I'm so honoured to have won…', and instead went straight into 'Hey everyone, I have a brag post today. I'm not even going to pretend that this is a humble brag. This is a flat out 'brag' brag. Are you ready? Here we go…' I went on to share my excitement and joy and held up a prop or two in the process. This post drew so many positive and supportive comments, even from people I didn't know. One woman wrote, 'I don't know this woman or how this video got onto my feed, but this is how women should share their successes. This video is a delight to watch and I am so thrilled for her. Women take note. This is a masterclass in how to talk about your achievements.' (You can watch the clip in your digital bonuses – just go to www.thegenderpenalty.com/bonuses.)

Playbook summary

The following is a summary of the attitudes and actions to help you adapt your play when you hit the Boasting penalty. To create your own personalised playbook, put a tick next to the strategies that resonate with you.

Pre-game attitude

☐ Remember that your words become their thoughts – steer the story that's most helpful for you.

☐ Boasting and boosting are both about visibility – one is just more palatable than the other. Don't miss the opportunity to boost your brand because you're not comfortable with bragging. They are not the same thing.

☐ You're not just telling people that you're awesome; you're reminding people that you exist. You are worthy.

On-field action

☐ Say 'Thank you' – then zip it!

☐ Claim and redirect.

☐ Use the words you want people to use of you.

☐ Dump the words that downplay, diminish or discount your abilities – true or not. Never play small.

☐ Keep a brag book.

☐ Share project wins and share the emotional credit of the good feelings that come with it.

☐ Praise others behind their back – your listeners associate good feelings with you and you both win.

☐ Be excited about your wins. Passion pulls people in.

Mantra: It's about boosting, not boasting. The greater my visibility, the greater my value.

Remember: It's not enough to be great; you have to be known for being great. This requires visibility. The better you get at stepping into the spotlight, the more opportunities you create and the more you amplify your impact.

Bonus: If you want your manager to know how to support you in the game, download the Coaches' Playbook for this penalty at www.thegenderpenalty.com/bonuses.

Personalised playbook for the Boasting penalty

What stood out to you from this chapter? What will you do differently as a result?

Use the following personalised playbook to record your ideas and commitments to yourself.

Insights

What resonated most with you from this chapter?

_____

_____

_____

Actions

What three actions will you take or do differently going forward? (With whom, in what context, by when?)

1. _____

_____

2. _____

_____

3. _____

_____

_____

Chapter 8

Penalty #4: Strength

To be taken seriously and seen as authoritative at work, women need to make tough calls, express unpopular opinions and push back on ideas. We also need to value our own time and protect our work boundaries, despite relentless pressure to please everyone else. For women, saying no and expressing strong opinions can be tricky territory that will quickly have us labelled as difficult or aggressive – whereas men showing the same behaviour are simply seen as strong.

Current play

What's going on with strong, assertive women? Why are they so vilified in the workplace and why is it so hard to set clear boundaries without penalty? What gives? How can women get the job done, if they can't hold firm boundaries? In this section, I explore the current game being played with respect to how men and women are allowed to show strength at work, and what happens when they do.

Assertive equals aggressive

We've all been there. You push back on something and get accused of being too aggressive, too harsh or too mean. Or you say no to someone and feel instantly guilty. Or you take a passionate stand against an idea and get told to calm down. But you're not upset and you're not being aggressive – you're simply in dialogue about the idea, like everyone else. As women, we are often held to a different standard when displaying strength and pushing back.

Research from Amy Cuddy of Harvard Business School, and colleagues Susan Fiske, of Princeton, and Peter Glick, of Lawrence University, showed women are judged as either likeable (warm) or competent (strong) but rarely both together.[49] If women are seen as overly warm, they are seen as pushovers or people-pleasers, and their value is discounted. If they are seen as too strong or highly competent, they are seen as difficult, aggressive or too direct. These women are the 'ball breakers', 'the ice queens' and the 'b!#ches'. Frustratingly, women must walk a constant tightrope between strength and warmth – always balancing the feminine and masculine stereotypes and not over-balancing too far in either direction, for fear of being misinterpreted. For men, it's a different story altogether. Be strong and you're a great leader. Be warm and you're a great leader. Same, same.

And it's not just that women get punished for showing strength, there's more; men get rewarded for it. Research from Yale University and Northwestern University concluded that angry behaviour from men was rewarded, but for women, it meant being labelled incompetent and untrustworthy of power.[50] We also know that women who negotiate their pay are seen as less likeable – and 30 per cent less likely to receive their pay increase than men.[51] And when women say no or don't accept offers of more responsibility (often without commensurate pay increases) they are seen as ungrateful and not a team player. Ouch!

A woman's work is never done

Without society's permission to push back as strongly or as often as men, women end up doing the work no-one wants to do. A study out of Harvard by business economics professors Linda Babcock, Maria Recalde, Lise Vesterlund and Laurie Weingardt, 'Gender differences in accepting and receiving requests for tasks with low promotability', found that women are 40 per cent more likely to be volunteered to do the non-promotable work than men (think: office housework). And the big twist in this research was that the managers who volunteered these women were both male and female. Yep. We're all part of society's conditioning. Added to this is the finding that women themselves are 50 per cent more likely to self-nominate for the work than men, if no-one else puts their hand up. Yep. Think about it. Who was the last person to clean up after a meeting, organise the office Christmas party, your colleagues' birthday card, the team lunch, the charity appeal, the office move? Was it a woman?

Whenever I pose this question to my keynote audiences and workshop participants, I always get a resounding 'YES!' For the most part, this is the work that women do. We are team players, we want to be helpful, we want to be supportive and a lot of us don't like to say no. Lucky for everyone else.

The upshot of taking on the less visible, less promotable and less valued work is that you miss out on opportunities to build your CV with real work, high-profile work and valued work.

> **The more you play the supportive role, the more you're supporting others to play the lead role, rather than you.**

Now this is not to say you can't do some of these things because you like to or even want to (or have to because it's actually your job), but let's start by making sure it's a choice, not an expectation. Let's make sure everyone does their fair share.

Summarising the Strength rules

'Say no.' 'Be firm.' 'Push back.' 'Stand up for yourself.' 'Be a leader.' 'Be more assertive.' 'Be more authoritative.' 'Ask for a pay rise.' 'Negotiate harder.'

Backlash from the Strength penalty

The following figure highlights the Strength rules and provides an example of the backlash in action. The external sources represent the backlash that comes from people around you (such as managers and colleagues) when you try to be stronger and firmer with those around you. The internal sources represent backlash that comes from your own thinking (based on your beliefs and perceptions), when you try to be stronger and firmer with those around you.

I've also provided further examples in the following bullets.

External:

- 'You're being difficult.'
- 'She's a ball breaker.'
- 'You're quite aggressive.'
- 'You're too direct.'
- 'She's too bossy.'
- 'You're too dominant.'
- 'You're putting people off.'
- 'Calm down. Don't get so emotional.'
- 'You're not a team player.'
- 'You're not being very helpful.'
- 'But you helped last time.'
- 'You're letting me down.'

Internal:

- 'I don't want to rock the boat.'
- 'I don't want to be difficult.'
- 'I'm being too pushy.'
- 'I'm being too harsh.'
- 'I feel too mean.'
- 'People won't like me if I'm too hard on them.'
- 'I feel too combative and controlling.'
- 'I'm too much for people.'
- 'I hate saying no to people.'
- 'I want to help as much as I can.'
- 'I feel like a b!%$# when I say no.'
- 'I don't want to come across as rude or uncaring.'
- 'I can't let people down.'

Doesn't hold people to account for crossing boundaries or not delivering.

Lets things slide, hoping they will work themselves out.

Stories from the field

Didi was an invaluable part of the team. She was well regarded by all who worked with her, including at the highest levels. As a result, she was given greater responsibility and more and more work. But Didi had a secret problem. She couldn't say no. And she was making herself sick by taking on so much work. Refusing to let any balls drop or compromise quality outcomes, Didi worked practically day and night – till early hours of the morning, and every weekend. She was even too busy to take leave.

Internal Backlash
from ourselves

Didi was overworking and began suffering from serious health problems. Eventually, upon the insistence of her partner, she went to see a doctor. The doctor said she was very ill and ordered her to have a week off. That was the only time off she'd had since she started – Didi was literally working herself to an early grave. After sharing some of her health problems and how desperately she felt trapped by her inability to say no, the women in our coaching group rallied. They enforced breaks by coming to collect her for lunch, they checked in on her throughout the day, they helped her to say no ... and survive. After a few weeks of some tough love and total support from the group, Didi reported that she had made some changes.

With the support of the sisters around her, she found the strength to leave her work phone and laptop in the car each evening so she wasn't tempted to check in on work. She left work at a reasonable hour and stopped working on the weekends. She also started adding conditions when she said yes. 'Yes, I can do that for you but I can't start until next month.' 'Sure, I'd love to help but you'll need to speak to management to bump their priority if I'm to work on this immediately.' 'Yes, I can start that today. What would you like me to stop in order to make time for this?'

The good news for Didi was that once she found the strength to say no (or yes, with conditions), to pushback and protect her ability to be at her best, others started responding in kind. They stopped giving her things that would take up her time just because she could do them. They saw how truly busy she was because she was prepared to show them. They helped her manage her time, by taking things off her plate because they wanted her to succeed. Helping herself gave others permission to help her also. But, of course, the most important outcome was that Didi soon reported a clean bill of health. All her stress-related symptoms due to overwork began to reverse. You could say that Didi literally saved her own life.

Adapting the play for Strength

Adapting the play is about changing your behaviour during the game – in this case, to overcome the Strength penalty. Being firm can feel mean, but only at the beginning. In time, showing strength and holding boundaries becomes a natural part of the game – a part you cannot do without. The following strategies will help you break the people-pleasing habit, once and for all.

Stay strong – say yes to yourself first

If women are supposed to be amenable, accommodating and supportive, then saying no becomes a problem. This usually translates into saying yes … to everything. Can you type up these notes for me? Yes. Can you do this report that's due at 5 pm today? Yes. Can you volunteer for this committee 50 kilometres from your home for no good reason other than we need another body? Yes. Wait. What?

The truth is when we say yes to others, we are saying no to ourselves – no to quality outcomes, no to our future opportunities, no to our professional reputation. When we take on too much work because we want to deliver on everything, we end up delivering on nothing. Oh, the irony. Our job as professionals is to get the job done. Prioritise your delivery. Say no to others and yes to yourself.

Pushing back feels like letting down – reframe the pain

Given the way women's strength is received, is it any wonder that standing your ground, sticking to your guns and pushing back can feel so challenging? No-one likes to say no to someone in need or not help out when they know they could. And that's the trap. You don't want to disappoint other people.

It's hard to say no to someone who has become reliant on your generous yes. It's hard to retrain people to share the non-promotable work when you're the only one who ends up saying yes. It's hard to stare into the eyes of disappointment and still feel good about yourself. But here's the thing. It's not about you. The disappointed face, the upset face, the grumpy face are all shades of the same face – the inconvenienced face. This is not about you not being nice enough to help someone out; it's simply about you not being convenient anymore. Your no means they have to do more work, their own work, or find someone else to do the work. This is an inconvenience – for them. But it's not a reflection on you, so don't take it personally.

Start to see disappointment as a sign of progress – a sign that you are making the right calls for you. Be prepared to disappoint people, to upset people and to inconvenience them. In fact, expect it. And be prepared to disappoint people for as long as it takes to establish the boundaries you need. It's time to reframe the pain as part of the game.

Give them what they want, mostly – say, 'Yes, and'

The easiest way to say no is to say yes. Stay with me. A no is abrupt and disappointing. A yes is easy and pleasing. So give people what they want … and then add what you want. It's a 'yes, and' approach. It works like this:

> 'Can you do the report for me today?'
>
> 'Sure. I'll need to clear some other things off my plate first. What would you like me to stop working on today while I get this report done for you? Here are the other things due today.' (Yes, I can do the work. And here's what I need to get it done.)

Often times, people who ask you to do things have no idea how much you've actually got on and who else is wanting those tasks from you. When you show them your workload and ask them to help you prioritise what to drop (read: who to disappoint), they are often quick to rescind their request or help you manage your workload. Either way, you are not taking on more work; you are taking on different work.

Another version of this is to say yes (for this time) and offer an alternative for next time. This is especially useful when retraining your work colleagues to share office housework. For example:

> 'So you'll take the minutes today, Sheryl?'
>
> 'Happy to. And then I'll nominate someone to do it next week. And then they can nominate the next person after that. Or we could set up a roster? What would work best?'

An even stronger version of saying yes to say no is a twist on the classic 'to-do list'. This strategy is more to keep yourself accountable for where you push back and where you lean in. It's called a 'to-don't list', and it contains things you've promised yourself you won't do anymore.

Sample to-don't list:

- Don't respond to emails immediately.
- Don't say yes without my 'and'.
- Don't take on projects that don't align to my career goals.
- Don't say yes out of guilt.

One of my clients has taken this principle a step further and used it to 'ring-fence' her agreed performance goals. Together with her boss, she formulated her team's deliverables for the coming year. It was a big stretch but her boss was adamant she get it all done. She said 'yes, and': 'Yes, we can do this, and here's what I need to make it happen. I need permission to say no to anything not aligned to these goals.' She then listed all the projects, activities and ad hoc requests that could potentially jeopardise the goals and that she and her team would need to say no to. Her boss agreed. Eventually, the day came when her boss asked her to send one of her team members to help out in another project. She politely declined. She reminded him about their agreement and talked through the consequences of losing her team member at this crucial time. The boss changed his mind. She remains on track to smash her goals.

Soften the blow – frame the delivery

At times, you will need to take a difficult stand, share an unpopular opinion or push back on someone else. What I'm talking about here is not just saying no to office housework. It's stronger and harder than that. As such, it's more about managing the backlash and changing the way people around you see women's strength. A great way to do this is with a framing statement. A framing statement is a line you add before the strong message, which shifts the way it is received. Here are some examples (with the framing statements in italics):

· '*At the risk of sounding emotional,* I can't believe we are still considering this option right now. It's ludicrous.'

· '*At the risk of being called a ball-breaker,* I repeat, where is the report I asked for five days ago? We can't deliver without that information.'

· '*Call me aggressive if you want,* but I disagree. This is not what the client wants and we should not be wasting our time on this initiative.'

· '*You'll no doubt label me as difficult for what I'm about to say,* but I won't have my team working on that project. We've been through this before and I haven't changed my mind. It's still a no.'

These framing statements allow you to acknowledge the stereotypes of women and stand strong anyway. It's about nudging the narrative and taking the wind out of the sails of that stereotype.

Leverage unconscious signalling – use strength cues

Another strategy to soften the blow of a strong message is to soften the message, but strengthen your non-verbals. For example, you may decide it's in your best interest to keep this person on side and not risk being seen as too strong. You need to pander to their position, power or status but you still need to get your message across. So you soften the message with hedging statements and tentative language and then use strong non-verbal cues to do the real work. (I know, I know. We've worked so hard to dump these weasel words but we have to adapt our play in the moment, right?) Here's an example:

- **Soft words:** 'You're right. We need to move on this ASAP. I'm wondering if we're missing something else here, though? Perhaps we could consider more options before jumping in? We might get caught out if we move too soon. What do you think?'
- **Strong signals:**
  - direct eye contact
  - head straight and not tilted
  - weight equally distributed on both feet – no rocking
  - lower tone (professional voice, not personal voice – think parent voice)
  - strong voice, no wavering
  - tonality down at the end of the questions so they sound like statements – cos they are ☺
  - expanded body posture – don't slump or shrink into the space.

The words are softened but the delivery is strengthened. And because our brains pay more attention to the non-verbal cues to interpret intentions (such as tonality and body language), we leverage the power of unconscious authority signalling. You're welcome.

Playbook summary

The following is a summary of the attitudes and actions to help you adapt your play when you hit the Strength penalty. To create your own personalised playbook, put a tick next to the strategies that resonate with you.

Pre-game attitude

☐ Each 'no' amplifies the power of a 'yes'.

☐ Reframe the pain and get used to disappointing others.

☐ Stay the course while others get used to your new boundaries and strength.

☐ The more you stand firm, the easier it will become.

☐ Stick to your guns. You pave the way for the next woman when you do.

On-field action

☐ Say 'no' more often.

☐ Give up the justifications and apologies – no is a complete sentence.

☐ Say 'yes, and'.

☐ Start a 'no club' with your buddies and report in on what you have said no to.

☐ Stop volunteering for office housework.

☐ Stop allowing yourself to be volunteered for office housework.

☐ If you do get volunteered for office housework say yes (one last time), and then start a roster to share the work around equally.

☐ Stick up for yourself.

☐ Ask for what you want.

☐ Ask for what you deserve.

☐ Don't work a full time-job in your part-time hours ... seriously. Just stop.

☐ Be playful with your strength – power can be soft as well as strong.

Mantra: When you say no to others, you say yes to yourself.

Remember: The more you take on, the less you can deliver on. Your desire for quality is compromised by quantity, so say no to others so you can say yes to yourself.

Bonus: If you want your manager to know how to support you in the game, download the Coaches' Playbook for this penalty at www.thegenderpenalty.com/bonuses.

Personalised playbook for the Strength penalty

What stood out to you from this chapter? What will you do differently as a result?

Use the following personalised playbook to record your ideas and commitments to yourself.

Insights

What resonated most with you from this chapter?

_____

_____

_____

Actions

What three actions will you take or do differently going forward? (With whom, in what context, by when?)

1. _____

_____

2. _____

_____

3. _____

_____

_____

Chapter 9

Penalty #5: Motherhood

Being a working mother is not for the faint-hearted. Always busy, always guilty, always too much to do and not enough time to do it. Women who work and have families are working around the clock, at two jobs. In most cases, this is not the plight of a *parent*, however; it is the plight of a *mother*. Added to that, when women have children, they become 'carers' and their commitment to work is questioned. When men have children, they become 'providers' and their commitment to work is expected.

And there is more to this penalty. Women are often caring for elderly parents as well as children. And then there are the women without children – women who can't have children, don't have children yet or chose not to have children at all. These women also face the motherhood penalty, albeit in a different way. I have included some backlash examples for these women as well.

Current play

Why are mothers treated differently to fathers? What's the real cost of being a mother? Is it possible to have both a successful career and a happy family, without guilt? And why, oh why are women still doing all the housework!? In this section, I explore the current game being played with respect to motherhood and the expectation of who does the caring.

Mothers are less committed ... apparently

Women pay a high price for being working mothers, because society generally cannot hold the reality that mothers can be both committed to their children and committed to their careers, equally. Granted, they often have to divide their time unevenly for a period of time, (because: boobs and food) but having love for a child doesn't mean losing love for your work, and nor does it necessarily change your commitment to either in the long run. Becoming a parent, however, does change the perception of your professional brand, and whether this change is for better or worse, depends on your gender. And, no, ladies, it's not good news for women.

When women have children, they are seen as less committed, but when men have children, they are seen as more responsible. And research undertaken in 2008 by Eden King of Rice University found that working mothers are believed to be 'less capable and mentally tough' compared to people without children.[52] As a result, women also receive fewer challenging assignments. Sigh.

This perception is heartbreaking for the women who are committed and determined to succeed in their careers. The women I work with report being very committed to their jobs – kids or no kids. And this bears out anecdotally in my discussions with many leaders who see beyond the stereotype. They share how great it is to have a mother on their team because they're focused, organised and hard-working. They don't have time for the office BS, they just get stuff done. Now, of course, some women decide to stay home and raise their kids (and let's celebrate this choice!), but it's not every woman's choice. In fact, contrary to what most people think (and confirmed by a massive study of Harvard Business School alumni) most women who leave their jobs after having children are not doing so because they want to stay home with their bubs. Rather, it's because their current work environment makes being a working mother simply too hard.[53] Just to be clear, it's often the system that doesn't support working mothers, not that the mothers don't want to work.

Caring is costing us

As sad as it is to admit, motherhood is costing women at work. Women who have children are more likely to be the primary care giver. As such, they will either take a career break or work part-time in order to raise their kids. This means less money comes in each week, lower pay and less superannuation (while fathers often still receive an unofficial 'baby bonus' in their pay checks). I mean it literally when I say care is costing us.

But the cost is more than dollars alone; it's also career prospects, networks, visibility and opportunities to get ahead. If you work part-time, you often don't get the same access to high-visibility or business-critical projects, because you are not spending enough time in front of the people who give out these projects. This means you get less experience to show on your CV, which affects your ability to get more of these opportunities, which ultimately affects your confidence and career prospects. And this is likely to only accelerate as more women choose a hybrid working model to support their families. I'm afraid out of sight will prove out of mind if managers don't learn to manage remote workers more inclusively.

Added to these costs of women being on a lower income is the choice that inevitably needs to be made once the kids are a bit older – about whether a mother continues to stay home with the kids or goes back to work full-time. Women typically earn less than men already, so chances are a mother will already earn less than her partner in a heterosexual partnership – and this is then compounded if she's taken a career break or worked part-time after having kids. When the decision about who should stay at (or go back to) work is made (read: who will bring in the most money for the family), it most often falls in favour of the man. Exasperating this situation is the enormous cost of childcare when mothers go back to work. The mother's income may be just enough to cover the childcare costs with little remaining. Or, worse, the family may be worse off because there is not enough to cover the childcare costs. This situation keeps women locked in the cycle of always staying home because it will never make economic sense for the family unit to live off her smaller salary. And this is why it's not always a 'choice' that women stay home as carers. It's an economic equation. And so the gender roles dig in their hurtful heels once again, and further entrench the gender pay gap.

Mothers don't fit the mould

It's readily acknowledged that the world of work was originally made by men, for men. And it never included women, let alone women with children. Women are trying to fit a mould that was never cast for them, and is not being recast quickly enough. The 'anywhere, anytime' performance model sets a standard of work performance that primary care givers, mostly women, can never hope to meet. This was also the number one obstacle for why senior women in the Asia–Pacific region felt unable to attain executive roles, as cited in 2018 research from McKinsey & Company.[54] The model assumes that employees will put work over family, are available to travel at a moment's notice, work long hours and usually have a 'wife' at home to look after the ever-present business of family life. But it simply doesn't work. Not for women, or men.

Enter the part-time solution. Mothers can't work full-time so they work part-time instead – all the while expecting that this will be enough to keep them on their path. But it isn't. It offers a bandaid solution at best. Part-time roles are still stigmatised as career holding patterns for those more dedicated to their family than their work. Added to this is the kicker of doing more, but getting less. A lot of women in my programs who work for part-time wages still do the equivalent of full-time hours (a well-researched phenomenon). Why? Let me count the ways! They feel guilty, it is an implied expectation, they don't want to be left behind in their careers, they don't want to become invisible, and the list goes on.

Author and expert on culture and equality, Michelle P King says it best in her book *The Fix: How to Overcome the Invisible Barriers that Are Holding Women Back at Work*, when she says,

> *Workplaces want men and women to work as though they don't have children. However, society requires that working mothers raise children as though they never work.*

The 'motherload'

Motherhood is a time of evolving identities, shifting roles, and a masterclass in the balancing act of home and work responsibilities. One of the biggest issues for working mothers is the mental load that accompanies the myriad daily activities required to keep a family together and hold a job down at the same time. The 'mental load of motherhood' describes the planning, structuring, organising, managing and monitoring that is required to keep kids alive and households running. This load usually falls on mothers, even when they work full-time (mostly because the pattern becomes set when they worked part-time and was never re-distributed).

The mental load of motherhood means that on top of women being 5.5 times more likely than their partners to do all or most of the house-work,[55] and doing up to three times as much unpaid care work as men (including elderly parents and relatives),[56] women are also organising all the daily activities required to run a household and a family. In her *New York Post* article, 'Millennial men want 1950s housewives after they have kids', journalist Jennifer Wright reports that 75 per cent of mothers assume responsibility for domestic appointments such as children's check-ups, and are four times more likely than their partners to miss work to care for sick children. Mothers are called by the school when the child is sick and needs to be collected. They are organising the meal plans, the kids' lunches, the play dates, the doctor's visits, the haircuts, the never-ending purchasing of new clothes, uniforms and shoes (seriously, can we get a share system going for new shoe requirements every six months!). They are managing a constant to-do list in their head at all times. Even when fathers are doing some of this work, mothers are often still organising it all.

The issue with the mental load is that at home we call it being a mother, but in the workplace these activities are called management. And they usually earn a pay premium for the increased responsibility – but for women at home, they only receive the extra 'tax' burden … without the pay increase. Mothers are doing two jobs and not being properly acknowledged or compensated for either. And that's why they're so goddamn tired. All. The. Time.

It is worth mentioning that COVID-19 did a brilliant job of spotlighting the plight of the working parent. We Zoomed into each other's homes and private lives, we shared the trials and tribulations of home schooling, and the role of the working parent finally took centre stage. However, we still have a way to go. Even during the COVID-19 pandemic, it was typically the mum who did the majority of the childcare or home schooling. And it was still women's careers that were most interrupted by the pandemic – because part-time workers were the hardest hit when the economy halted. The motherload was acknowledged, but the burden wasn't shifted.

Summarising the Motherhood rules

- 'You can have it all. Work and a family!' (Congratulations, you now have two jobs and less pay.)

- 'Congratulations! You're having a baby. We'll support you.' (Doesn't support you.)

- 'Your job will be here when you get back.' (It isn't and you're made redundant.)

- 'Motherhood won't jeopardise your career prospects.' (But no executives here work part-time, or job-share, or work flexibly …)

- 'You're still on track for Partner.' (But we reassigned all your big clients while you were on mat leave …)

- 'You can work part-time and have lots of time at home.' (You can work your full-time job in 'part-time' hours and do all the stuff at home, too.)

Backlash from the Motherhood penalty

The figure overleaf highlights the Motherhood rules and provides an example of the backlash in action. The external sources represent the backlash that comes from people around you (such as managers and colleagues) when you try to be a working mother. The internal sources represent backlash that comes from your own thinking (based on your beliefs and perceptions) when you try to be a working mother.

I've also provided further examples in the following bullets.

External backlash for mothers:

- 'Our team meeting is on your day off. You don't mind dialling in, do you?'
- 'We discussed that on Friday when you weren't here. It's too late to change now – the decision has been made.'
- 'How can you be on the road so much? Who's looking after your kids?'
- 'Your job was made redundant while you were away.'
- 'I've given the account to Bob since you'll be on maternity leave soon and then coming back part-time.'
- 'I'm not sure you can handle the responsibility.'
- 'Is your husband babysitting your kids while you're on this assignment?'
- 'Why are you so stressed all the time?'

Internal backlash for mothers:

- 'I'm a bad mother.'
- 'I'm a bad employee.'

- 'I feel guilty when I'm not with my kids.'
- 'I feel guilty when I'm not at work.'
- 'I'm trying to keep up with everything but I feel overwhelmed.'
- 'I'm just grateful to have another job, even if it's half my pay and half my ability.'
- 'This is full-time work for part-time pay, but at least I'm employed.'
- 'Why do others make it look so easy?'
- 'Why can't I keep on top of it all?'
- 'I'm exhausted. All. The. Time!'

It's worth noting that women without kids can also face backlash.

For example, the external backlash for women without kids includes:

- 'Sally can do it. She doesn't have kids like everyone else. She's ambitious like the rest of us!' (Read: she's a man.)
- 'When are you going to have kids?' (Read: why is it taking you so long to have kids? Or when are you leaving us?)
- 'Why don't you want kids?' (Read: what kind of woman doesn't want kids?)
- 'Why haven't you had kids yet?' (Read: what's wrong with you that you can't have kids?)
- 'Congratulations on your wedding. It's only a matter of time before you have kids!' (Read: everyone who gets married has kids … don't they?)

Internal backlash for women without kids includes:

- 'Why do I have to pick up all the slack on school holidays?'
- 'What if I want to take holidays over school holidays too? Just because I don't have kids doesn't mean my needs are any less important than the needs of parents.'
- 'I feel ashamed. I'm desperately trying to have kids but nothing is working. It's exhausting pretending I'm okay with it all.'

- 'Once I got my career sorted, I tried everything I could to have kids but it was too late for me. I'm devastated. I don't want to talk about it because I don't want to be pitied.'

- 'There's nothing wrong with me because I don't want kids. I can still be caring and loving and nurturing without being a mother.'

Stories from the field

Keely was a Partner at a professional services firm, about to go on maternity leave for the fourth time in ten years. As part of our coaching work together, she shared with me that the last three times she had returned from maternity leave, she found it difficult to reclaim her main clients – who had been looked after by other partners while she was away. Not only that, but as she was winding down to go on leave, it was also considered standard practice for any potential clients to be redirected because 'she was going to be away'. As a result, each stint on mat leave saw her partner portfolio decrease considerably in size, requiring her to essentially rebuild it almost from scratch. Every. Time. She. Returned. She'd had enough – and not just for herself, but also for other women who faced the same challenge. This time she vowed it would be different. And so our strategising began.

We reviewed what had worked, and what hadn't, in the past. We made lists of actions to take, when to take them, who to involve and why. She listed all her clients and allocated different caretakers to each group. Then she met with each client and their new caretaker for a formal handover meeting, where she was explicit in the roles and expectations of caretaking, time frames of return and regular oversight check-ins from her during her months away. She met with her boss and outlined her plan and her expectations of what would happen on her return. She documented the caretaker list so others knew who was looking after her clients while she was on leave.

She appointed a maternity leave buddy who would keep her updated with relevant work changes and organised a rotation of monthly coffees with each partner to stay connected to (and visible to) her peers and the firm. By the time we were done, she had a clear action plan to retain her clients, save her portfolio and, better still, change the mindset of the broader business around caretaking of portfolios for women going on maternity leave. She was very happy to be 'keeping connected on my own terms' and to have a clear direction and strategy. She also felt proud to be leading the charge and making real changes on supporting women partners taking maternity leave.

When Keely returned to the office ten months later, she hit the ground running. Rather than needing to rebuild her portfolio, she met with each caretaker and was updated on the status and needs of her clients. She then organised meetings with her clients and the caretakers to officially take back the work. By changing the mindset from 'reallocation' to 'caretaker', Keely was back on track in no time. She was once again working at a level that is expected of an experienced partner with a hard-earned portfolio.

Keely told me, 'We have a special relationship with most of our clients and it takes time and effort to earn their trust and show them that they can rely on us 100 per cent. Having to hand over those relationships in the past really hurt, and sometimes resulted in women feeling like they needed to be back in the office working much sooner than they otherwise would have liked. Empowering myself to take a stance and set clear expectations that, while I was incredibly grateful for my colleagues stepping in to take care of my clients when I was on leave, I will be back to further invest in that relationship. Returning to work this time around has been a much more positive and productive experience and I am committed to ensuring this is replicated throughout the organisation.'

Adapting the play for Motherhood

Adapting the play is about changing your behaviour during the game – this time, to overcome the Motherhood penalty. While it can feel like just another thing on your to-do list, setting clear expectations from the beginning will save a lot of extra effort in the long run. (And by effort I mean housework ☺) The following strategies will help you challenge the status quo of parenting expectations and get the most out of being a mother and a career woman.

Mothers are undervalued – flip the script

Just because society undervalues the role of mother, doesn't mean we have to. If you are a working mother, you are a leader. Make no mistake about it. One of my male clients once said that he'd learned more about leadership by being home with his young daughters for six months than he ever did in the workforce. If you can negotiate breakfast with a toddler day in and day out, you can handle people and personalities at work, any day of the week.

What do you learn from parenting that is transferable to the work-place? Let's see … how about:

- adaptability
- budgeting and finances
- creativity and innovation
- empathy and emotional intelligence
- high-pressure negotiations – with unreasonable and overly emotional tiny stakeholders
- hope and optimism
- influence and persuasion
- motivation and engagement
- operating in chaos – with no handbook
- resilience
- resourcefulness
- time management and productivity.

Need I go on?

We need to remember that the skills of parenting are some of the most enduring and critical skills any professional will develop in their working life. That's not to say you can't develop these skills without being a parent. Of course, you can. But you do get a masterclass when you become a parent.

> **Motherhood is not a penalty; it's a boot camp for brave leaders. If you can be a parent and survive, you can be a leader and thrive.**

The 21st century version of leadership is calling forth the adaptable, creative, resilient, emotionally intelligent and committed. That is a working parent. That is a mother. We can win the game of work by embracing the motherhood card and leveraging its strengths in the game of work. We can fly the flag of experience in transformational leadership qualities whether we've had experience of this in the workplace or not. I say to women all the time, if you can deal with children fighting in the playground, you can deal with conflict in the workplace. The players may look different, but the game is the same. And you've done the training. You're ready to go.

Accepting is condoning – resist the easy path

The unrealistic expectations, the financial cost and the lack of career opportunities that working mothers face is not okay. Part of the problem with these working conditions is the more we accept them, the more we condone them and the longer they are here to stay. It's like a worker who wants to prove themselves – but does so by working over-time, all the time. In the process, they create unrealistic expectations of that role. They never get more resources or support because management has now been trained to expect one person can handle the role on their own. So when mothers work full-time hours in part-time roles, for example, they are training the company that this is okay, that it is reasonable and that this is the norm ... and so it is.

Being the first one to push back on unrealistic expectations can be hard (see the Strength penalty in chapter 8 for help) but if everyone is doing it all the time, it's no longer about you. It's about the company. The pandemic has taught us that companies that are not listening to their people and what they want are losing their people. Companies that are still mandating five days in the office are out of step with the market and the market is voting with its feet ... right out the door. The same will happen for companies when women start challenging pay rates, expected hours, lack of opportunities and lack of support – the company will either rise to the challenge or lose good women in the process. If Keely didn't take a stand for what she expected to happen while she was on maternity leave, she would have lost all her clients again. But she no longer allowed the past to determine her future.

This goes for your home life as well. Review the emotional load of managing, organising and planning your family's daily lives. Explore the household chores and responsibilities and get your family involved in divvying them up. (Use the Fair Play card deck to help make it fun – see www.fairplaylife.com/the-cards to find out more.) If you are used to doing everything because you used to have more time (and now you don't), it's time to re-evaluate the household duties. It may be an uncomfortable conversation to have with your partner or kids, but for the sake of your mental health and wellbeing, do it. You need a break. And if you think no-one will do as good a job as you do, ask yourself how this belief is serving you. Is the perfectly stacked dishwasher really that important? Really? And if you have a family who are already doing their equal share, then celebrate them every day. Encourage them to talk about your household arrangement with others, to normalise this model of family living.

Playing small controls the stress – break the habit early

In order to keep their sanity, working mothers must make difficult decisions. Do I focus on my career or do I focus on my family? A vote for one feels like a vote against the other. And when push comes to shove, the family usually wins out, at least at the beginning. So women often start playing small at work. We choose safe assignments, push others forward, and take a back seat with our careers to focus on our family. And then we forget to re-evaluate. Playing small becomes a habit. Instead of challenging the structures that make it hard to take on better jobs in fewer hours and more meaningful assignments with less experience, we let ourselves stay small. It's easier. And let's face it – there aren't many examples of successful part-time female executives to model … yet.

Working mothers don't hold themselves back from opportunities because they fear failure; they hold themselves back because they fear success. Success brings yet another level of pressure, of stress and of responsibility which for many women is simply not worth it. But the key to remaining ambitious and in contention is to not limit your prospects but limit the expectations of how to fulfil your prospects. It's about setting clear boundaries and negotiating realistic outcomes and expectations. This is what allows you to say yes to the bigger opportunities, with full confidence that you can handle the pressure and the workload ahead.

Don't limit your ambition; manage others' expectations.

The presence of guilt – embrace it

With so much to be responsible for, balls will drop. And it will feel like failure. You will always have too much to do and not enough time to do it. Enter the guilt. The never-ending, always present, guilt. Guilt for not being with your kids, guilt for not being at work, guilt, guilt, guilt! The trap with guilt is that you can become a hostage to its grip. You think you can appease it or ease it if you just do more of this or less of that. You think it will go away. It won't. Nor does it need to.

The presence of guilt means you care. And that's a good thing. Think about it. If you didn't feel guilty about missing work or not being with your kids, it would mean you don't care anymore. So as long as you care about your work and your kids, you will wrestle with guilt. Full stop. So stop fighting it and start embracing it. But only briefly; it's a visitor, not a resident. Don't catastrophise, and don't give it anymore airtime than it deserves. Show it the door before it sits on the floor, and get on with your day.

Quality over quantity – be present

You've no doubt heard the mantra quality over quantity. But I doubt you've heard it applied to being a mother! And yet that's exactly what I'm suggesting you focus on. Rather than trying to be all things at all times, recognise that you'll be more effective if you compartmentalise the two roles. It's not always possible, granted, but it's liberating when it is. If you're at work, be at work. If you're at home, be at home. Give yourself permission to spend more quality time with your kids than quantity time with them. Kids know when you are 'phoning it in', when you're there, but not really there. So give up the ruse. You may end up spending 'less' time with them but they will have a better experience when they are with you. And that's got to be better than nothing? The more focused you are in the present, the more effective you become in the moment. And remember – you can also play the long game. You don't have to take on everything at once. Sometimes family comes first and the job takes a back seat. And that's okay too.

Visibility creates opportunity – be seen

In the Boasting penalty (chapter 7), I talked about the importance of being visible in order to get picked to play. This was about reputation, beyond your presence. In this section, I'm talking about your actual presence – literally being seen. Being invisible is an issue for those who work part-time because, well, part-time. If you are only there part of the time, you are only top of mind part of the time. Managers are busy, and reminding them that you exist, that you do great work, and that you should be considered for that big opportunity is important for building your career. If you never go into the office on the same day as your boss, but your colleague is in there every time your boss is, the boss will know them better. They will see more of their work, build greater trust, have more time to chat about opportunities, and will be more likely to think of them when that opportunity comes up. It's as simple as that. Visibility creates opportunity. Be seen.

The COVID-19 pandemic added a nuanced complexity to this issue for women. Flexible work has allowed women to ease the pressures of juggling both roles but, in doing so, has created a double-edged sword by making it easier for them to stay away from the office. If you're not going into the office as often, be sure to find creative ways to stay front of mind with your manager and colleagues. Create reasons to have a video call. Pick up the phone for a quick check-in. Send a thank you note. Don't let out of sight become out of mind.

Adapting the play for motherhood

The following is a summary of the attitudes and actions to help you adapt your play when you hit the Motherhood penalty. To create your own personalised playbook, put a tick next to the strategies that resonate with you.

Pre-game attitude

☐ Stop playing small – create clear expectations instead.

☐ Remember the skills of motherhood are transferable – honour this by using them at work.

☐ Celebrate the capability of other working mothers – raise their profile and performance.

☐ Make friends with guilt – but don't give it too much air time.

On-field action

☐ Talk up the capability and productivity of other mothers – start shifting the perceptions.

☐ Tell your work what you need – for example, no meetings during school pick-ups and/or more interesting work.

☐ Negotiate pay rises even when you're part-time.

☐ Expect promotions even when you're on maternity leave.

☐ Divvy up household tasks – including the emotional and mental load (planning, organising, structuring and managing).

☐ Outsource at home and at work – as much as you can.

☐ Delegate more (at home and at work) – ask 'who else could do this?'

- ☐ Ask for help – remember it's not babysitting if they're the father – it's parenting. ☺

- ☐ Prioritise self-care – take naps, take walks, eat well.

- ☐ Let go of the unimportant stuff.

- ☐ Embrace the guilt and stay present in the moment.

- ☐ Stay connected during mat leave (if you want).

- ☐ Challenge assignments that aren't utilising your full potential.

- ☐ Create clear boundaries on part-time hours and part-time workload.

Mantra: Motherhood is not a penalty; it's a boot camp for brave leaders. Step into this value and leverage your experience.

Remember: Motherhood magnifies obstacles and opportunities. Strategise your play to optimise your game. You've got this.

Bonus: If you want your manager to know how to support you in the game, download the Coaches' Playbook for this penalty at www.thegenderpenalty.com/bonuses.

Personalised playbook for the Motherhood penalty

What stood out to you from this chapter? What will you do differently as a result?

Use the following personalised playbook to record your ideas and commitments to yourself.

Insights

What resonated most with you from this chapter?

_____

_____

_____

Actions

What three actions will you take or do differently going forward?
(With whom, in what context, by when?)

1. _____

_____

2. _____

_____

3. _____

_____

_____

Now that we can celebrate and leverage the skills and abilities of motherhood, it's time to leave the gender penalties behind us. Each of the plays in the chapters in this part has paved your way up the Gendered Career Ladder and closer toward your rightful place at the top – invaluable. You now have strategies to speak up, be visible, showcase your strengths, stand for what you believe, say no, push back, and juggle competing roles of work and motherhood, with grace and grit. And every time you adapt your play in the moment, you become more nimble on the field and better equipped at navigating the gender penalties.

You're now ready for the final level. It's time to explore the power plays that advance the game for good.

Notes

PART III

THE POWER PLAYS FOR ADVANCING THE GAME

Leila worked as the senior HR manager for a large retail company. She was excellent at her job and always delivered results. Eventually she reached a point in her career where she was ready for a change. She wanted a new challenge. Her boss was trying to fill an operations manager role at the time, so she put her hand up. She had never been an operations manager before but she knew what the job entailed and she knew she could do it. However, her boss disagreed. He said she didn't have the right experience and, therefore, he didn't think she would be seen as a credible candidate in the eyes of the Board. She didn't get the job.

Over the course of the next few years, she watched as three different operations managers came and went, without delivering what was required. After watching this go on from the sidelines, Leila decided to try again. She knew her boss was getting desperate. Maybe now he would be ready to give her a shot? She was right. He was. She finally got the job.

Needless to say, she nailed it. Not only did she smash her targets, time and again, but when she eventually left the role, her legacy lived on. She did such an outstanding job of leading her team to greatness, that to this day people still say, 'What would Leila do in this situation?' Leila is now in an executive role where she gets to shape the way managers view employee potential. She has used this experience to introduce policies and practices that benchmark employees against competency frameworks (not perceptions). This means the decision to employ someone is not solely reliant on how much experience they have, but rather what transferable skills and competencies they can objectively demonstrate. Bravo!

Leila's story is a great example of both adapting the play and advancing the game. In her career, she had travelled quickly up the Gendered Career Ladder (refer to chapter 1), adapting her play and moving through the Invisible, Compliant and Competent stages early on. She landed squarely and firmly in the Credible camp, waiting for a chance to prove herself Invaluable. It took courage to convince her boss to see beyond his conditioned expectations of her and put her in that role. But once he did, her real journey began. She was able to amplify her impact and pay it forward by introducing a new hiring policy that changed the game for good. She adapted her play in the moment while 'on the field' and changed the rules in the long term in order to advance the whole game. That is what a power play looks like.

Now that you're familiar with the state of play (how the current game is being played) and the gender penalties (what's holding women back and how to adapt the play in the moment), you're almost at the top of the Gendered Career Ladder. You're on your way to breaking through the conditioning and ready to rally your courage and take your final steps past the Credible rung and onto Invaluable. It's time to amplify your impact, and advance the game for good.

Advancing the game is no small feat. It takes a power play to make it work. A power play is a way to win bonus points or gain an advantage in a game, in order to fast-track success. In the game of work, it's about ensuring that a change for *you* is a change for *all*. It's about standing up to the status quo, challenging the current culture and finding your voice in a sea of strong opinions. We know how important women's contributions are. We know how effective their leadership is and how valuable their perspectives are. It's time to leverage our strengths. It's time to enact our power plays.

In the chapters in this part, I explore five key power plays that can help you advance the game for good. Here we go.

Chapter 10

Start where you are

Despite celebrating many encouraging initiatives right now, watching the pace of the gender equality movement limp along (and in some places go backwards) can be disheartening, frustrating and at times overwhelming. We – women and men – still have so much left to do, and we're making such slow progress. Sometimes you might feel powerless to effect change, but you must remember great power can come in simply starting where you are. Rome wasn't built in a day and neither was the path to gender equality. It was paved one brick at a time – through one conversation at a time, one meeting, one initiative, one moment. Making progress is about getting started – *lots* of people, at the same time, getting started together. This is how we pick up the pace of change.

In this chapter, I provide some strategies that can help you start where you are and reshape the game.

Start with your superpowers

Everyone is brilliant at something. The more you work to your strengths, the greater your impact. So what are you great at? What are your strengths, your passions and your capabilities? Make a list of these superpowers and create any excuse to use them more often. If you're great at rallying people and passionate about childcare, lobby for childcare facilities in your workplace. If you love connection and conversation, volunteer to interview men and women about their flexibility experiences at work and showcase them online. It doesn't matter what you do. Just do more of what you're good at. It's the easiest way to make a difference.

Take my client Angela. Angela decided to take her passion for fitness and wellness and start a Global Step Challenge at her work. On the surface, this initiative may not be about gender, but it challenged gender norms, nonetheless. Angela's initiative got great traction across the broader business. It catapulted her into the spotlight with senior executives, including the CEO. She was credited with starting a company-wide wellness movement, and inspiring others to do similar things. The company saw a woman lead an initiative, showcase her strengths, put herself out there, co-ordinate a large project and demonstrate her unique style of leadership. Seeing more and more women take the lead teaches society that we can, and we should, expect more women to take the lead.

Take small, steady steps

The quickest way to start where you are is by taking baby steps. Ask questions, start conversations, share observations. You don't have to launch the next #heforshe campaign or give the next Julia Gillard 'Misogyny Speech' in order to have an impact on the game (although you certainly could!). You can start small by noticing what is happening around you on a daily basis. Ask where all the women are on male-only panels, leadership teams and committees. Give feedback on policies and procedures that are difficult for women at your workplace. Challenge assumptions about what female customers value and give your perspective as a female consumer. Use your voice, vote with your feet, make it count.

This is what Jackie did in a marketing meeting with a group of other employees. They were reviewing the latest add campaign on the screen, which featured an image of a woman doing yoga … in a bikini. Jackie spoke up: 'I've never done yoga in a bikini before. I've never seen any of my friends do yoga in a bikini either. Why is this model doing yoga in a bikini? Who is our target market for this ad?' The target was women, but the group said they hadn't really thought about the bikini. On reflection, they agreed that it wasn't appropriate. The model was removed. The campaign was changed. All it takes is one voice to point out the obvious and away we go. Baby steps can create big impacts. Put your shoes on. We're off.

Share your stories

Tell your own story – to men, to your boss, to your organisation. Share your experience as a woman with people who need to hear it. Don't assume it's just you, because you know that it's not. Use your confidence and clarity and share your experiences to serve the greater good. Share your insights, perspectives and experiences. And share them often.

Jarna saw the need to involve more men in her organisations' efforts towards gender equality. She knew how powerful sharing stories could be, and took it upon herself to 'reverse' mentor her current executive mentor. He would mentor her about working in the business and she would mentor him about gender issues in the business. In their conversations, she shared what she had learned from our training, what challenges women faced in the organisation and what needed to be done to change it. She employed her storytelling superpower and turned her mentor into a passionate ally for gender equality. He couldn't believe some of the things he had learned from her and became personally engaged in the topic. He appeared on a panel discussing 'male allyship' that was beamed to all employees globally, and started asking other country departments what they were doing to support women at work. And all this came from the power of story.

Be your own role model

When we're advancing the game, we are by definition breaking new ground. That means it's very likely that you will be the first, the only or one of the few to be challenging the current game. If you're waiting for a role model to show you the way, don't despair if they're not there. Be the role model you seek. In 1913 Mahatma Ghandi said, 'If we could change ourselves, the tendencies in the world would also change' – commonly now paraphrased to 'Be the change you seek in the world'. Take this advice. You are the role model you have been waiting for.

In episode 68 of one of my favourite podcasts (*The Doctor's Farmacy* with Dr Mark Hyman), I heard an interview with the founder and CEO of The Freshglow Co, Kavita Shukla. Kavita invented a product called FreshPaper, which is a small biodegradable sheet of paper that can be dropped into any existing packaging, fridge drawer or fruit bowl, and keeps your fruit and veg fresh for two to four times longer. It's a brilliant product used by individual consumers through to large retail chains. At the time of writing, FreshPaper is in the process of being made available to roughly 1.2 billion people who lack access to refrigeration. Just incredible! What struck me about Kavita's story (apart from her decision to tackle this global food waste problem – because, well, why not?), was what she said right at the very end of the interview. Talking about what her entrepreneurial journey had taught her, she said,

> *When I first started, I didn't have anyone that I could look to that made me believe that I could do it. You know, I've never seen a woman inventor or CEO or an entrepreneur that looked like me. [A young, short, brown woman.]*

She continually received messages that in order to make her company successful she would need to find someone with at least 20 years in the food industry (which she didn't have), and someone with the skills to build a company (which she also didn't have ... yet). So she discounted herself for 10 years. She calls this time the decade of doubt, when she didn't believe that she could be the best person to bring her ideas to the world. But she was wrong. And her thriving company, driven by her compelling vision to take on the global challenge of food waste, is testament to her true abilities and determination. She didn't have role models with her background or experience. But she didn't need them. She became her own role model and, in the process, a role model for millions of aspiring female entrepreneurs like her. She started where she was. So can you.

Start where you are power play summary

- Use your strengths to get into action.
- Start with small, steady steps.
- Tell stories about your experiences.
- Be your own role model.

Chapter 11

Challenge the norms

Normal is a construct of what is common, not necessarily what is right. In a world of conditioned gender norms, it's easy to think that what exists around us has been deliberately constructed rather than unconsciously accepted. Too often we accept the status quo because we don't realise we're in it or that we can change it. It just feels … well, normal. But by choosing to advance the game, we are choosing to challenge these norms. The more we see, the more we need to say. And after reading this book, no doubt you will have a lot more to see. You need to ensure you don't fall into step with the current players on the field – because silence is often compliance. Remember the rousing words of Lieutenant General David Morrison of the Australian Army in his 2013 speech: 'The standard you walk past is the standard you accept'. (In 2016, Morrison attributed these words to former Chief of the Australian Defence Force David Hurley.) And so it is with the status quo. The more we stay trapped in what is, the more we stay silent about what could be. It's time to speak up. It's time to stand up. It's time to shake things up.

In this chapter, I provide some strategies that can help you challenge the norms and change the game.

Look in the mirror

It's easy to think the work of change needs to be done by others – by your organisation, for example, or by society. But the truth is it needs to be done by all of us. We need to be able to look in the mirror and challenge the part we play in holding the status quo in place. It's not always fun, but it's always worth the effort. Remember – we are all caught up in society's conditioning.

Recently I caught myself slap-bang in the middle of my own gender bias. I was buying some new camera equipment from a big electronics retailer and I was looking for a sales assistant to help me. I saw the sign to the camera area, saw a female sales assistant standing right under the sign – and then looked past her in search of 'someone who could help me with my camera equipment'. I spotted a man in the adjacent area and walked purposefully toward him to ask for his help. He responded by walking me over to the female sales assistant I had just overlooked. Me. The author of this book. The woman who has conversations *every day* about gender equality and how women are *overlooked by society*. Not by me. I'm a feminist. But by 'society'. I was ashamed and red-faced as I listened to her expert advice and selected the product she suggested. Lesson learnt … again.

> Before we challenge others, we must be willing to challenge ourselves. No exceptions.

And starting with your own behaviour is not just about how you behave with others; it's also about how you behave towards yourself. Brené Brown is a social researcher, storyteller and worldwide phenomenon. She's the author of multiple best-selling books, the presenter of one of the top watched TED Talks of all time, and busy professor, teacher, podcaster and keynote speaker. In May 2022, she made a brave announcement on her podcast *Dare to Lead*. She said that for the first time in her career, she would be taking three months off – completely. Not three months off from the podcast, but full steam ahead on everything else, I mean three months off from *all* work. She hit the pause button on everything, including all social media. She said coming off the back of the pandemic years, and running full out in her businesses, she was tired. Her staff were too. She knew she set the policies for those around her, so she set a new one: a break.

This was one of the biggest examples I'd seen about challenging our own expectations. She said she was nervous about cutting herself off so completely. What if the business was dead when they got back? What if they lost subscribers? What if, what if, what if? In the end, none of it mattered more than their collective health and wellbeing. Full stop. What personal habits, beliefs and behaviours are no longer serving you? What can you change about the way you work that shatters the stereotypes of society? Do it. I dare you.

Review policies

Policies and procedures in the workplace provide the cultural guard-rails for accepted behaviour. They are not always right, but they are always in place. If something doesn't feel right or make sense to you, chances are it's not right for a lot of others as well. We only need to look (again) to our sporting arenas to see this in action. In July 2021, the women's Norwegian beach handball team were fined 150 euros each by the European Handball Federation. Why? They boycotted their regulation bikini bottoms for shorts – closer to the kind the men are allowed to wear. They had repeatedly complained about this uniform inequality since 2006, but no-one was listening. They'd had enough, and it was time to challenge the norms. They wore the shorts anyway, making headlines around the world. Even the singer and songwriter Pink offered to pay their fines for them in a sign of sisterhood solidarity. By November that year, the global backlash from the ridiculous rule was overwhelming. The social pressure started by these courageous women had done the trick. The women's uniform requirements are now more in line with the men's – long tops and long shorts, and no bikinis or midriffs in sight.[57]

Women's game uniform as mandated by the International Handball Federation – before and after the protest from the women's Norwegian beach handball team

Before   After

Not even a year later, in June 2022, another uniform debate played out around the world. This time it was about the white uniform required by all tennis players competing at Wimbledon, one of the four major Grand Slam tournaments in tennis and the oldest tennis championship in the world. Some of the female players said they were not comfortable to wear white during the toughest, most gruelling matches of their lives, on national television ... when they also had their period.[58] Imagine that. You're in tight white. You're playing sport. The whole world is watching ... and you have your period. So, why white? What is so important about wearing white to play at Wimbledon? Is it for safety, athleticism or performance reasons? Nope. It's about tradition – and the Victorian-era idea that any sign of sweat was improper and rude, with white clothing believed to minimise the visibility of sweat and cool the players. That's it. It's important to wear white – well, because, it's 'proper', and that's what we've always worn. Women's pesky needs be damned. Time to challenge the norms ...

In the corporate world, a great example of common policies that need revision exists in recruitment. We need to ensure they are fair for everyone. This means challenging the old 'tap on the shoulder, you've got a new job' approach, and ensuring equitable and transparent policies are in place. Men and women should be on the shortlist, as well as men and women on the hiring panel, and a policy that years of experience shouldn't overshadow qualities and transferable skills – and so on. It's time to audit these old policies and procedures and make them work for everyone.

Be aware of practices

If policies are the guardrails that keep us on track, our daily practices are the behaviours that determine whether we choose that track. They are the implicit behavioural norms that create the culture we work in. Your organisation may have a policy of paternity leave for men, but how many men actually take it up in practice? A difference can emerge between what is supposed to happen and what actually happens. Having policies that support gender equality are pointless if our daily behaviours aren't aligned.

Tracy experienced this very issue. One day, she posed a very important question in our coaching group: 'Anneli, what do I do about the meetings that happen after the meeting? The one where the men all get together, without the women, and make different decisions to the ones made as a whole group?' She shared that her executive leadership team ran inclusive and effective meetings (those that were robust and safe, with all voices valued). However, once everyone left the meeting, the men would often gather again in another location and rehash the meeting – often behind closed doors in one of their offices, or at a coffee shop nearby. Tracy didn't think they were doing it to purposefully exclude the women. These were good guys, just catching up after a meeting.

But their practice of gathering together after the main meeting served to undo the inclusive nature of that meeting – especially if they then changed the decisions that had been mutually agreed to in the larger group. It was creating tension in the office, and Tracy wasn't the only woman asking this question.

After being coached by the group, Tracy decided on her course of action: she would gently insert herself into these 'after meeting' meetings. She didn't feel the situation warranted a direct conversation, because the men had no malicious intent to exclude women. But rather than let the situation continue, she chose to use her presence to nudge it in another direction. This one small shift helped to close the gap between the practice of exclusion after the meeting and the policy of inclusion during the meeting. If she was in those after meetings, she could ensure the conversation didn't turn into a new meeting or new decisions weren't made without including everyone else.

So what did she do exactly? A number of things … She attended every executive meeting in person (rather than virtually) so she couldn't be cut off from the after-meeting conversation. She deliberately stayed in the boardroom after the meetings finished so she was already part of the after-meeting conversation. When the men left the room to continue their conversations, she was right there with them. In the end, she found that not every after-meeting conversation was focused on the content of the last meeting, but when it was, she was right there, nudging the narrative of inclusion.

Another good example of a clash between policy and practice came from a woman who told me she was reluctant to try out for a store manager role. At her store, they sold heavy household equipment and had a big stockroom out the back where they housed all the products. A common perception in the organisation was that women couldn't be effective store managers because they couldn't move the equipment in the stockroom. While this inability to move large equipment might be true for some women (and some men), it's also a great practice to challenge. The policy says that anyone can be a manager but, in reality, barriers exist that affect some individuals but not others. This is the perfect opportunity to create a change that would be better for everyone. In fact, that's exactly what this company has since done. As a result of these types of issues being raised by women, they now have electronic machinery that can move around the equipment, reducing the need to rely on strength – and the potential for injury. This is a win for everyone.

What needs changing in your workplace? These changes could include those that perhaps the people in power aren't privy to, don't see or don't experience – but you do. Maybe it's a need for childcare or parental leave, or a review of how work assignments are divvied out, how team building golf days and boozy bar nights are decided on, or maternity leave (on ramping and off ramping), superannuation rules or promotion rates. Maybe it's gender stereotypes – championing strong women and supporting sensitive men. What do you know about? What do you want to bring about? What do you want to change? It's time to shake up the status quo.

> ## Challenge the norms power play summary
>
> - Look in the mirror – be the change you want to see.
> - Challenge existing policies and procedures – don't settle for the norm.
> - Always question default behaviours – if you see something, say something.

Chapter 12

Brave the backlash

Every time we adapt our play and go against our prescribed stereotypes, we open ourselves up to backlash. And this is even more so the case when we're attempting to advance the game by changing it altogether. In chapter 3, I outline how backlash is the whistle that blows when you are playing out of bounds. It's society's negative reinforcement when you are not playing by the rules – or the right rules. It can be tough. It can be harsh, unfair and uncomfortable. And yet it is the fear we must face as we push ourselves to the next level.

This chapter provides strategies that can help you brave the backlash as you strive for change.

Brace for impact

When pushing for change, no doubt you will ruffle some feathers. It's inevitable. You must brace for the impact of your strong stance and press on anyway. Remember the story about Jess whose colleague was constantly restating her ideas in their team meetings (refer to chapter 6)? She gave him the feedback about his behaviour and he changed his ways to be more mindful in meetings. What I didn't tell you back in chapter 6 was that in between sharing the feedback and him actually changing his behaviour were two days of silent treatment. Two days. Two full days. No hi or hello, no good morning or goodbye. Nothing. This is pretty confronting backlash when you sit opposite someone day in, day out, as Jess did.

Luckily for Jess, this man was a supporter of gender equality, was open to the feedback (eventually) and was a decent guy prepared to do the right thing. He just needed time to process the feedback and work through his own discomfort – which he did. Jess stayed strong through this backlash because, despite her own discomfort, she knew it was part of the change process. And so she braced for impact.

Bounce back after a blindside

Sometimes the backlash occurs without you directly creating it. You may not have asked for the change, but you have to put up with the resulting backlash all the same – mostly because you benefit from it, so you become a natural target for it. Take the case of quotas or targets. As soon as the mandate is set, the backlash begins. 'You just got that job because you're a woman.' 'Men can't get promoted anymore; we may as well leave.' 'We can't get the best person for the job anymore. We have to hire a woman.' Despite research suggesting how effective quotas are at getting more women into leadership roles – and how effective those women then are in the roles – it's not always easy for the women promoted under these directives. If the men (and women) in the organisation are not sold on the business case for this, they struggle to back the initiative. This leaves women at the mercy of kneejerk reactions and unfair perceptions. They become blindsided by the backlash they didn't ask for or expect.

Take Ashlee's example. When Ashlee was promoted to lead her current team, one of her team members (now her ex-peer) complained to her boss. 'She just got this role because she's a woman. She shouldn't be in this role. She doesn't have enough experience.' He responded to her leadership with underwhelming support. This is subtle but still hurtful backlash and Ashlee felt blindsided. Luckily for Ashlee, her boss supported her appointment and pointed out all the ways she was the best candidate for the role and why she got the job. And, no, it wasn't because she had the most experience in this function but because she had the best leadership qualities to build a strong team and outperform in the role. Ashlee decided to bounce back from this blindside by simply doing the best job she could. After a few weeks of seeing Ashlee in action, the resistant team member did a complete 180 – and even apologised to her directly. 'I'm sorry I misjudged you. You are the best person for this job. I can see that now.' Nice.

If you are a quota appointment, don't turn down the role because you don't want to receive special treatment. Say yes and do the best damn job you can. Prove to others that you may have received support to get the role, but you are achieving success because you are competent – plain and simple. In time, the process of your appointment will fade away beneath the backdrop of your brilliant results. And now you've made it easier for the next woman. Bravo.

Another example of how to bounce back from unexpected (and uninvited) backlash comes from a post I saw on my LinkedIn feed recently. An assistant project director shared that an older male from her professional network had suggested ('jokingly') that she may have found herself in her current role due to diversity targets. Sigh. Rather than letting this get her down, she bounced back and put a post on LinkedIn with her response. Without mentioning any names, she outlined what had happened and offered this response:

> *Thanks mate – it's perhaps also the 17 years I spent getting an education, including an academic scholarship to a private high school, the engineering degree I achieved first class honours for (interestingly, the exams weren't graded on diversity), the thesis I wrote that won a university award (no gender criteria there either) and the years I have now spent working hard when I need to, taking risks to pivot my career, strategic decision-making about my chosen career path, hours spent with mentors and colleagues to guide my career path, my excellent CV, my enthusiasm, ambition and even just some general skill and experience.*

Mic drop. Boom.

Let your values guide your response

Sometimes backlash is so abrupt and so disconcerting that you need to dig deep into your values to stand against it. You have to remember who you are, what you stand for and what you believe in to give you the courage to hold your ground.

Melissa was a new manager, finding her feet and working to build strong relationships with new stakeholders. To her disappointment, she'd been having difficulty with one of her organisation's main suppliers. He was a strong personality who was treating her poorly and speaking to her unprofessionally. Even though she was new, she was more junior and he was one of the companies' biggest suppliers, she'd had enough. In their next client meeting, he spoke to her unprofessionally and made yet another unrealistic demand. This time she responded directly. Calmly and confidently, she said, 'I don't appreciate the way you are speaking to me or the emails you are sending. What you're asking for is unrealistic and I'm not going to commit to it.' He was shocked.

After the meeting, the supplier proceeded to make a complaint about her. He spoke to her boss and their General Manager, and threatened to go to the Director as well. She stood her ground. She called her boss and the supplier's boss and explained to both of them what happened and why she'd acted as she did. Both of the managers were supportive of her and agreed his behaviour was unprofessional and unacceptable. This young manager anchored her response in her values, as a leader and as a human. For her, it was unacceptable to treat another person the way he was treating her – seniority, power or status aside. Her values enabled her to brave the backlash for doing what was right, no matter the cost.

This is how you speak truth to power. This is how you brave the backlash.

Don't personalise the pain

Backlash can feel like a personal attack, because at some level it is. It is you who is experiencing the negative response to your actions. But while the backlash is directed at you, it's never really about you. It's about a role in society that you happen to represent in that moment. And it's more about the other person and how they are being affected than it is about you. You need to distance yourself from the backlash response and see it from a new perspective.

In a strange way, backlash is something to be celebrated. Without it, we are not making waves, not challenging the status quo and not making change. The very presence of backlash is a tick for trying. You can't get a foul in the game if you're not chasing the ball. Avoiding backlash is easy if you stay small, play nicely and keep your head down. But that's not our way now, is it? We know too much. We've seen too much. We want more.

Brace yourself for the backlash, know that it's not about you, celebrate it as a sign of progress, and play on.

Brave the backlash power play summary

· Brace for impact when you push against the status quo.

· Bounce back from a blindside by standing strong in your achievements.

· Let your values give you the courage to stand strong.

· Know it's not personal, even when it is.

Chapter 13

Create the new

Once we start questioning the norms around us, we realise how much opportunity exists for meaningful change. As women, we have an informed perspective about what we need. *You* have an informed perspective. Think about it. What would make your life easier at work? A creche? A four-day work week? More job-sharing? What about life in general? How about phones that actually fit into your hand? Or more female toilets in pubs, clubs, bars, theatres, restaurants, conferences – *anywhere*, really? Or clothes with more pockets? Or any pockets?! (Is this just me?) We are in the world every day and we have a perspective. The important question is this: what are you doing with yours?

In this chapter, I provide some strategies that can help you create the new game … if it's still a game at all.

Fill the gap

As women, we know what's missing in our experience. We know when we are not being represented in media, when products are not made for us or when the world reflects values we don't hold. And instead of trying to convince others to take a risk on a new product, a new project or an unproven market, we can do it ourselves.

Reese Witherspoon's mum once said to her, 'If you want something done, honey, do it yourself.' She wasn't talking about office housework, of course; she was talking about creating what you want in the world. For Reese, this was more opportunities for women in film – including more women-led projects and women-driven content. Reese saw a gap in the market, and she was sick of waiting for Hollywood to start embracing women – so she did it herself. The industry gasped and said no-one would watch films about women, by women. There was no market for it. There would be no funding for it. They were wrong – except for the funding part – they were right about that. Undeterred, Reese and her business partner started their own production company, Pacific Standard, with their own money (because, funding issues). You may know some of their early work: *Gone Girl*, *Wild* and *Big Little Lies*. You'd recognise these productions because they were hits. And they were hits because Reese saw a gap in the market and she went for it.

Entrepreneur Kristy Chong tells a similar story of filling the gap. The founder of Modibodi started her company in 2013, researching and testing new fabrics that would allow her to launch a ground-breaking, category-creating product – leak-proof undies. After giving birth to her second child, Chong suffered from unmentionable and inconvenient leakage while training for a marathon. She knew she wasn't alone in her predicament and searched for an underwear product to support her needs (rather than bulky pads). She found nothing. So she created one – enter ModiBodi leak-proof underwear. In 2022, her company sold for AU$140 million. 'If you want something done, honey ...'

And then there's the story of Lumi Interactive, a gaming start-up founded by Lauren Clinnick and Christina Chen. In distinct contrast to some potentially violent, competitive and socially confronting video games, they created a new one called Kinder World. This is a game where players take care of unique virtual houseplants. It's built off the ideas of compassion, community and supporting others as you look after yourself. The idea came out of the dark days of the pandemic lockdowns, where they witnessed the power of every day kindness on individual and collective wellbeing.

Given the types of games on the market, a game that focuses on kindness was certainly a gap that needed to be filled. And their investors agreed – to the tune of a record-breaking, seed-round funding of US$6.75 million dollars. Oh yeah!

And don't be disheartened if you don't fancy yourself as an entrepreneur, hungry to start your own business. Much innovation is needed within our corporate cultures. Intrapreneurs are just as important as entrepreneurs. We need players inside companies, researching, innovating, creating and launching new products and initiatives. Whether it's supporting new flexibility policies or new office layouts with childcare areas, or pushing for the four-day work week (come on, we can do this!), we need your perspective.

If you experience a gap, challenge yourself to fill it.

File the edges

While creating something brand new can be thrilling, re-shaping something that currently exists can be just as rewarding. If the current way of working doesn't fit the female mould, we can file the edges to make it fit. Whether it's reinventing how industries operate, or chang-ing the existing structures that don't work for women, we have the opportunity to create the new, by re-moulding the old.

Another great example is the visionary brilliance of multi-award-winning lawyer Marianne Marchesi. Marchesi is the founder and Managing Principal of law firm Legalite. Described as a 'legal innovator and disruptor who has dared to do law outside the traditional model', Marchesi is redefining what it means to practise law. Not only is her firm challenging the status quo and simplifying legal services (so regular humans can follow along – fist bump, sister!), but she also offers a transparent, value-driven pricing model and a focus on wellbeing in law. However, the most important part for women is that she has created a genuinely flexible work environment that allows all staff to integrate their personal and work lives. By flipping traditional ideologies on their head, she filed the shape of her law practice to better fit the needs of each individual – irrespective of their gender, ability or background.

Create a new game

Sometimes, even more is needed than filing the edges. Sometimes, it's not just tasks and roles that need recreating but whole businesses. Leading into the global financial crisis/subprime housing market collapse, a group of female Icelandic investment bankers grew to be appalled at the risky and rash financial decisions being made at their company and in the Icelandic economy (and the rest of the world). For them, the writing was on the wall. The kind of cowboy, hypercompetitive, risk-taking investment decisions they were seeing were going to get the companies (and their clients) into major trouble.

So in 2007 they started their own business – Audur Capital. They based their investment business loudly and proudly on female investment values – including risk awareness, profit with principles, care, due diligence and caution. By the end of 2007, most of the Icelandic financial companies had collapsed and three banks had been nationalised. Audur Capital was one of the few Icelandic financial companies left standing. They had an informed perspective. They didn't like the industry they were a part of, so they changed it.

Create the new power play summary

- · Fill the gap and dare to dream of a better way.
- · File the edges and recast the existing moulds.
- · Challenge yourself to create a new game.

Chapter 14

Work together

Perhaps you've heard the quote, 'Coming together is a beginning, staying together is progress, and working together is success' (attributed to Henry Ford and Edward Everett Hale). Changing the game of work takes all hands on deck. With decades of intractable policies, procedures and practices keeping our cultural norms in place, we need to muster as much help as possible to shift the system we're in. We need people from all backgrounds, all industries and all walks of life, stepping in to lend a hand. When shifting the game of work, everyone is welcome. Plus, it's more fun, effective and motivating to tackle this challenge with other dedicated change-makers.

This chapter provides some strategies that can help you work with others to create a compelling future for all.

Amplify other women

The best way to break bias is to expose people to the truth. Women are great leaders, women are talented performers and women can be strong and direct – and should not have to smile so that others will listen. The more we see these strong, talented, decisive women out front, the more we normalise their presence. So one of our jobs in the sisterhood is to shine the light, spread the love and stand by each other when boldly challenging the norms. This means bragging on behalf of other women, and speaking about their accomplishments and achievements. It means getting more women onto stages, presenting in meetings, taking the lead on high-profile projects. It means showcasing women in non-traditional roles doing non-traditional things.

Amplifying women is about spotlighting the value of women, wherever we can. The more we see it about, the more we bring it about.

A practical example of this is how we can support women's voices in meetings. When women are being interrupted, ignored or cut off (or having their ideas stolen), they need back up. Enter the echo chamber (or 'amplification' – thanks to the female staffers during Barack Obama's presidency for this strategy[59]). The echo chamber is where women (and men) add extra support to what a woman has just said. At least two or three other people will repeat an idea that was first offered by a woman and give them credit for it. This amplifies both the idea *and* the person who contributed it. This makes it harder for the idea (and the woman) to be overlooked and ignored – or the idea credited to someone else.

Another example of women supporting women comes from leadership expert Dr Kirstin Ferguson, who in 2017 unexpectedly created a global movement on Twitter. Sick of the way women were being trolled and abused online, she decided to showcase the amazing lives and stories of the everyday woman. And so #CelebratingWomen was born. Dr Ferguson committed to celebrating two women from anywhere with any background, on Twitter, every day in 2017. She asked them a series of questions about themselves so people could learn about their lives and hear their stories. It went viral. By the end of 2017, Dr Ferguson had profiled 757 women, from 37 different countries. Now that's how you amplify other women.

Leverage collective strengths (and stand strong together)

One of the strengths women are known for is collaborating. Women working together can cause an avalanche of action by sheer weight of focused attention and stubborn determination. It's easy to ignore one voice, but harder to ignore a chorus. Take the story of the women from Greenham Common, who played an instrumental, but (until now) little known, role in bringing about the end of the Cold War.

In 1981, a small group of women sat around a kitchen table in Wales, deliberating about what they could do to protect their children from the threat of nuclear war. The British government had just agreed to host American nuclear weapons at an airbase in Greenham Common in Berkshire (a county west of London). The women were worried that the missiles would make them a target during a nuclear war and put their children's lives at risk – and so they came together to do something about it. Their aim was to get rid of the nuclear weapons from their country. They decided on a protest march, from the Welsh capital, Cardiff, to the airbase in Greenham Common. They walked for 32 hours. It wasn't enough.

They realised they would need a bigger, bolder gesture to get more attention and have any chance of making a difference. So they set up protest camps around the airbase. The movement quickly grew, from 250 women protesting in 1982 to 70,000 women protesting in 1983 – no small feat in an era pre-dating social media. In time, women from around the world would set up their own 'Greenham Women Everywhere' protests to add their voices. The protesters faced innumerable hardships over the years, but they remained focused on their goal and committed to standing strong together.

Eventually, their dogged determination and untold sacrifices paid off. In 1987, leader of the Soviet Union Mikhail Gorbachev signed the Intermediate-Range Nuclear Forces (INF) Treaty with US President, Ronald Reagan. Soon after, more than 2600 land-based missiles were removed from Eastern and Western Europe and the two men were lauded as heroes for leading the world to peace. And yet, tucked away in obscurity is a video clip of an interview with Mikhail Gorbachev after the event – a clip that puts the work of the women of Greenham Common squarely at the centre of the peace deal.

In the clip, a reporter asks Mr Gorbachev how he was able to trust President Reagan to keep his end of the deal. He replies, 'I knew the women of Greenham Common would hold him to his word'. The cold war ended, in no small part, because a group of women bandied together to make a stand for what was right. A world without nuclear weapons. A better world for their children. A better world for humanity. Anthropologist Margaret Mead is widely quoted as saying, 'Never doubt that a small group of thoughtful, committed citizens can change the world; indeed, it's the only thing that ever has.' When women work together, we can change the world.

As inspiring as the women of Greenham Common story is (and it is!), we don't need to flip back through the annals of history to find evidence of women making waves together. It's still happening today. In 2022, a record number of women ran as independents in the Australian federal election. Known as the 'teal' candidates (sometimes dismissively), these independent women mobilised a nation to unseat the traditionally 'safe seats' of some of the country's biggest political players. Even though they were not from the same party, they had many similar goals – with a big one being to bring the voice of the people back into parliament. They aligned on key issues of climate change, integrity in politics and gender equality. Together, their independent voices shifted the balance of power in Australian politics.

Work with men

Working together to change the game is not just about women working with other women. It's about everyone working together. Men play a crucial role in changing the game; after all, they are in charge of most of it. They also have as much to gain from the changes as women do. Men are facing their own gender stereotypes and unrealistic pressures that keep them locked in their roles. If we want the changes that are better for everyone, and we want them to stick, we need to enrol all players in the game. This means sharing our perspectives and experiences with men – bosses, brothers, fathers, colleagues and team members. It means telling our stories and engaging men in frank dialogue about what they can do to help, even if it's uncomfortable – especially, if it's uncomfortable.

Tina joined the coaching group with some good news. Before the workshop, she had been feeling overworked, overwhelmed and under-appreciated, especially at home. She said she didn't feel confident speaking with her husband about it because she had always been the one to take on those duties. She felt guilty for sharing her stress. But arming herself with the knowledge that it wasn't just her experience, and that many women shared it, gave her the confidence to raise the topic. She shared what she had learnt, she shared her insights and realisations and she shared her concerns. In the end, her husband was very supportive. It turns out that he didn't realise she was under so much pressure and said he was happy to do more around the house and support the running of the family. Tina learnt an important lesson with that pivotal conversation. She learnt to ask for help. She told her husband what she needed and he stepped up.

It's too easy to think that solving gender bias is about supporting women alone, but it's about breaking all gender stereotypes. Men can help women break gender bias by picking up non-traditional roles in the workplace – such as the office housework, the part-time role, the paternity leave role, the emotional support role. When we no longer expect one gender over another to perform certain roles or duties, our work will be done. Until then, we need to smash as many stereotypes as we can to keep pushing forward.

Let men know the importance of their allyship, and be clear that imperfect allyship is better than passive perfection.

We'd rather men make a clunky attempt at supporting women than a perfect attempt at being a bystander. It's okay to make a misstep if you are genuinely offering support. Our role is to make sure men feel safe to make a mistake and say the wrong thing, and to challenge their own perceptions if their intentions are sincere. Men are our allies. They are our teammates on the field. Together, we can change the game for good. And if you need a way to help them get across the basics of gender equality, consider giving them my book *When Men Lead Women: Navigating the Facts, Fears and Frustrations of Gender Equality as a Male Leader*. It's the very reason I wrote it. (Shameless plug that I won't apologise for – you can grab a copy at www.anneliblundell. com/books.)

Work together power play summary

- Amplify other women, always.
- Leverage collective strengths and stand strong together.
- Work with men.

Conclusion

What's next?

Congratulations. You've arrived at the end of this book. We've covered a lot of ground together, so let's do a quick recap. In this book, I've explored the current game being played and why women are being left behind in the classroom, while men are scoring goals on the field. I've outlined why the rules are so confusing for women (answer: they were meant for men) and why we are still stuck playing this old game (answer: unconscious conditioning that entrenches the status quo). Then I unpacked the five gender penalties that create the biggest obstacles for women at work – namely:

1. Confidence

2. Communication

3. Boasting

4. Strength

5. Motherhood.

In each penalty chapter, I covered the state of play and the strategies to adapt to that play to turn obstacles into opportunities and stay on the field. And finally I covered the five power plays to advance the game for the long term:

1. Start where you are
2. Challenge the norms
3. Brave the backlash
4. Create the new
5. Work together.

And now here we are. You've got your personal playbook for how to win at the game of work, in your own way, on your own terms, for your own benefit (which, of course, helps everyone). Now it's time to amplify your impact and change the game for good.

All things considered, this is an amazing time to be alive. There is so much opportunity and so many ways women can change this world. I wonder what you've been inspired to do as a result of reading this book. Where do you want to make a difference? What's taken hold in your heart as you've read through the chapters? Maybe it's standing up for respectful conversations in our parliament, or solving critical climate issues, or closing the gender data gap or pay gap, or designing products, services and equipment that cater to all shapes and sizes. Whatever it is, we need that special something that only you can bring to the world.

And as you begin, let me offer one last thought …

My hope for you

Beyond the knowledge and insight you have gained throughout this book, I also want you to walk away from our time together with a feeling. In fact, not just one feeling, but all the feels.

I want you to feel:

- **Assured** that your experiences are normal – that you are normal *and* you are incredible. Keep being you.

- **Validated** that you belong – that the world has space for you. Stand up and claim your place.

- **Proud** that you've come this far. Every step counts. You've got this.

- **Excited** about your career path going forward. You have your personalised playbook, play full out.

- **Inspired** by the stories of progress we're making. Because we are making progress. Each and every day. Spread the word.

- **Grateful** that you are not alone. You have the wind of a million women at your back and the support of many men too. The world is full of good people. Together, we will make a difference.

My hope is that you feel seen and heard and, most of all, valued. I also hope that you experience true belonging and acceptance in this world, because that is humanity's greatest gift. It's what lights us up, it's what lifts us up and it's what makes us more of who we are. When we embrace and amplify our authentic self, we give others permission to do the same.

When we feel seen, we are more able to see. When we feel heard, we are more able to hear. And that's a game-changer.

Imagine a world where everybody feels visible, and where all voices are valued and all perspectives matter. This is the world I want. And I want to create that world with you. Let's do this.

Bonuses and next steps

Digital bonuses

Let the learning continue!

Throughout this book, I've referenced the bonus content available on my website dedicated to the gender penalties.

Here you'll find the following resources:

- **The Coaches' Playbook:** The guide to help your manager fend off the gender penalties you might face at work.

- **The Gender Penalty Quiz:** To see which penalty you need a stronger strategy for overcoming.

- **The Chick Chat Club:** Guided discussion questions to facilitate reflection and learning with a group of friends or colleagues.

- **Other bonuses:** Including cheat sheets, summary checklists and videos.

To claim your goodies, visit www.thegenderpenalty.com/bonuses or scan the following QR code.

And if you're ready for the next level, be sure to check out my online programs here, including the crowd favourite Credible Communication – Making your value visible. www.anneliblundell.com.

Corporate workshops

Want to bring the power of gender equality to your organisation? Anneli offers Women@Work, Applied Allyship, and Coaching Skills for Inclusive Leaders programs, as well as executive mentoring and keynote presentations. For more information visit www.anneliblundell.com/womeninleadership.

Let's advance the game together.

Get in touch

To find out more about working with Anneli, visit her website at www.anneliblundell.com, or get connected via the following:

- **LinkedIn:** @anneliblundell
- **Twitter:** @AnneliBlundell
- **YouTube:** @AnneliBlundellTV/videos

Endnotes

1   Harvey, W (2017) 'Gender differences in policing: A consideration of care ethics', Master's thesis, The University of Tennessee, Chattanooga, Tennessee.

2   Catalyst (2020) 'Why Diversity and Inclusion Matter'.

3   McKinsey & Company Social Sector Office (2010), *The Business of Empowering Women*, McKinsey & Company.

4   Gallup, Inc (2015) *State of the American manager: Analytics and advice for leaders*.

5   Wood, R (2013), *Building a Case for Gender Diversity*, Centre for Ethical Leadership.

6   Russell, J (2015) 'Female entrepreneurs are "more successful than men"', *Elite Business Magazine*, 17 August.

7   Heilman, ME & Hayes, MC (2005), 'No credit where credit is due: Attributional rationalization of women's success in male-female teams', *Journal of Applied Psychology*, 90, no. 5: 905–26; Hayes, MC & Lawrence, JS (2012), 'Who's to blame? Attributions of blame in unsuccessful mixed-sex work teams', *Basic and Applied Social Psychology*, 34, no. 6: 558–64.

8   Roman, I (2019), 'How policewomen make communities safer', TED Talks News and Politics.

9   Kim YJ, Engel, D, Williams Woolley, A, Yu-Ting Lin, J, McArthur, N & Malone, TW (2017), 'What makes a strong team? Using collective intelligence to predict team performance in League of Legends', in proceedings of the 2017 ACM Conference on Computer Supported Cooperative Work and Social Computing (CSCW '17), *Association for Computing Machinery*, 2316–2329.

10 Turban, S, Freeman, L, Waber, B (2017), 'A study used sensors to show that men and women are treated differently at work', *Harvard Business Review*, 23 October.

11 Correll, SJ, Benard, S, & Paik, I (2007), 'Getting a job: Is there a motherhood penalty?' *American Journal of Sociology*, 112(5), 1297–1339.

12 Player, A, Randsley de Moura, G, Leite, AC, Abrams, S & Tresh, F (2019), 'Overlooked leadership potential: The preference for leadership potential in job candidates who are men vs. women', *Frontiers in Psychology*, 10: 755.

13 Sanders, M, Zeng, J, Hellicar, M and Fagg, K (2017), *Advancing Women in Australia: Eliminating Bias in Feedback and Promotions*, Bain & Company/Chief Executive Women.

14 ibid.

15 ibid.

16 Correll, SJ, Simard, C (2016) 'Research: Vague feedback is holding women back', *Harvard Business Review*, 29 April.

17 ibid.

18 Fox, C (2017), *Stop Fixing Women: Why Building Fairer Workplaces is Everybody's Business*, NewSouth Publishing.

19 Wenneras, C, Wold, A (1997), 'Nepotism and sexism in peer-review', *Nature*, 22 May; 387(6631):341–3.

20 American Psychological Association (2005), 'Men and women: No big difference', 20 October; Tinsley, CH, Ely, RJ (2018), 'What most people get wrong about men and women', *Harvard Business Review*, May–June.

21 Fox, C (2017), op. cit.

22 ibid.

23 Bain & Company (2014) 'The crisis of confidence: How women lose faith in their career opportunities' infographic, 17 June; Coffman, J & Neuenfeldt, B (2014), *Everyday Moments of Truth: Frontline Managers Are Key to Women's Career Aspirations* report, Bain & Company, 17 June.

24 Fox, C (2017), op. cit.

25   Kay, K, Shipman, C (2014), 'The confidence gap', *The Atlantic*, May.

26   Karpowitz, C, Mendelberg, T, & Shaker, L (2012), 'Gender inequality in deliberative participation', *American Political Science Review*, 106(3), 533–547.

27   Shore, L (2017) 'Gal interrupted: Why men interrupt women and how to avert this in the workplace', *Forbes*, 3 January.

28   Tannen, D (1994), *Talking from 9 to 5. Women and Men at Work: Language, sex and power*, Virago Press.

29   Fox, C (2017), op. cit.

30   Chemaly, S (2018), *Rage Becomes Her: The Power of Women's Anger*, Simon & Shuster UK Ltd, p. 156.

31   Tatman, R (2016), 'Google's speech recognition has a gender bias', *Making Noise and Hearing Things* blog, updated July 2020.

32   Chemaly, S (2018), op. cit, p. 157.

33   ibid p. 189.

34   ibid p. 156.

35   ibid p. 158.

36   ibid p. 156.

37   ibid p. 156.

38   Menzies, F (nd), 'Gender bias at work: The argument for gender diversity targets', Culture Plus Consulting.

39   Terrell, J, Kofink, A, Middleton, J, Rainear, C, Murphy-Hill, E, Parnin, C, Stallings, J (2017), 'Gender differences and bias in open source: Pull request acceptance of women versus men', *Peer Computer Science*, 3: e111.

40   Sanders, M, Hrdlicka, J, Hellicar, M, Cottrell, J & Knox, J (2011), *What Stops Women from Reaching the Top? Confronting the Tough Issues*, Bain & Company/Chief Executive Women.

41   Goldin, C, Rouse, C (1997) 'Orchestrating impartiality: The impact of "blind" auditions on female musicians', National Bureau of Economic Research, January.

42 Steinpreis, RE, Anders, KA & Ritzke, D (1999), 'The impact of gender on the review of curricula vitae of job applicants and tenure candidates: A national empirical study', *Sex Roles* 41, nos. 7–8: 509–28.

43 Wenneras, C, Wold, A (1997), 'Nepotism and sexism in peer-review', *Nature*, 22 May; 387(6631):341–3

44 Correll, SJ, Simard, C (2016) 'Research: Vague feedback is holding women back', *Harvard Business Review*, 29 April.

45 Wosinska, W, Dabul, AJ, Whetstone-Dion, R & Cialdini, RB (1996) 'Self-presentational responses to success in the organization: The costs and benefits of modesty', *Basic and Applied Social Psychology*, vol 18, pp. 229–242.

46 Fox, C (2017), op. cit. p. 83.

47 Player, A, Randsley de Moura, G, Leite, AC, Abrams, D, Tresh, F (2019), 'Overlooked leadership potential: The preference for leadership potential in job candidates who are men vs. women', *Front Psychol*, Apr 16;10:755.

48 Heilman, ME & Hayes, MC (2005), 'No credit where credit is due: Attributional rationalization of women's success in male–female teams', *Journal of Applied Psychology*, 90, no. 5: 905–26; Hayes, MC & Lawrence, JS (2012), 'Who's to blame? Attributions of blame in unsuccessful mixed-sex work teams', Basic and Applied Social Psychology, 34, no. 6: 558–64.

49 Cooper, M (2013), 'For women leaders, likability and success hardly go hand-in-hand', *Harvard Business Review*, 30 April; Cuddy, A, Kohut, M, Neffinger, J (2013), 'Connect, then lead', *Harvard Business Review*, July-August.

50 Brescoll, VL, Uhlmann, EL (2008), 'Can an angry woman get ahead? Status conferral, gender, and expression of emotion in the workplace', *Psychological Science*, 1 March.

51 Thomas, T (2022), 'Women who ask for pay rise less successful than men, UK poll reveals' *The Guardian*, 4 April.

52 King, MP (2020), *The Fix: How to Overcome the Invisible Barriers that Are Holding Women Back at Work*, Simon & Schuster UK.

53 Fox, C (2017), *Stop Fixing Women: Why Building Fairer Workplaces is Everybody's Business*, NewSouth Publishing.

54 Woetzel, J, Madgavkar, A, Sneader, K, Tonby, O, Lin, D, Lydon, J, Sha, S, Krishnan, M, Ellingrud, K, & Gubieski, M (2018), *The Power of Parity: Advancing Women's Equality in Asia Pacific*, McKinsey & Company, 23 April.

55 McKinsey & Company (2017), *Women in the Workplace 2017*, McKinsey & Company/Leanin.Org.

56 King, MP (2020), op. cit.

57 Gross, J (2021), 'Handball federation ends bikini bottom requirement for women', *The New York Times*, 1 November; *ABC News* (2021) 'International Handball Federation reverses decision to force women's beach handball players to wear bikini bottoms' *ABC News*, 1 November.

58 Elias, Michelle (2022), 'Female tennis stars detail anxiety of being forced to wear "Wimbledon whites" during their period', *SBS News*, 6 July; MacSwan, A (2022), 'Protesters at Wimbledon urge end to all-white dress code due to period concerns', *The Guardian*, 10 July.

59 Eilperin, J (2016), 'White House women want to be in the room where it happens', *The Washington Post*, 13 September.

Resources and further reading

Resources listed in order of mention in chapter.

Chapter 1

Chamorro-Premuzic, T (2019), *Why Do So Many Incompetent Men Become Leaders? (And How to Fix It)*, Harvard Business Review Press.

Zenger, J, Folkman, J (2012), 'Are women better leaders than men?' *Harvard Business Review*, 15 March.

Zenger, J, Folkman, J (2020), 'Research: Women are better leaders during a crisis' *Harvard Business Review*, 30 December.

United Nations Entity for Gender Equality and the Empowerment of Women (UN Women) (2020), 'COVID-19 and women's leadership: From an effective response to building back better', policy brief no. 18.

Desvaux, G, Devillard, S (2008), 'Women Matter 2: Female leadership, a competitive edge for the future', McKinsey & Company.

Chapter 2

Elgin, S, H (1993), *Genderspeak: Men, Women, and the Gentle Art of Verbal Self-Defense*, John Wiley & Sons.

Shibley Hide, J (2005), 'The Gender Similarities Hypothesis', *American Psychologist*, September.

Tannen, D (1994), *Talking from 9 to 5. Women and Men at Work: Language, sex and power*, Virago Press.

Chapter 3

Uhlmann, EL, Cohen, GL (2005), 'Constructed criteria: Redefining merit to justify discrimination', *Psychological Science*, 1 June.

Chapter 4

Groysberg, B (2022), personal communication, discussing the findings from his research with thousands of Wall Street analysts over many years.

Koren, M (2019), 'The original sin of NASA space suits: They were never designed to fit everyone perfectly', *The Atlantic*, 27 March.

Weitering, H (2019), '1st all-female spacewalk scrapped over safety concerns, not sexism', space.com, 28 March.

Crabb, A (2021), '100 years of 'firsts': The story of women in Australian parliaments started with a blunder from an inept man with a not-quite-so-ingenious plan', *ABC News*, 13 July.

ABC News (2021), 'VIDEO: Women had to fight for the right for their own bathroom in Parliament', 12 July.

Partridge, E (2015), 'Loo coup: Women protest about lack of toilets at NSW Parliament', *The Sydney Morning Herald*, 28 October.

Purcell, E (2015), 'Women are protesting about the toilets in NSW Parliament House', *MamaMia*, 30 October.

McKinsey & Company (2015), *Women in the Workplace 2015*, McKinsey & Company/Leanin.Org.

Chapter 5

Desvaux, G, Devillard, S, Labaye, E, Sancier-Sultan, S, Kossoff, C, de Zelicourt, A (2017), *Women Matter: Time to Accelerate*, McKinsey & Company, October.

Sanders, M, Zeng, J, Hellicar, M & Fagg, K (2017), *Advancing Women in Australia: Eliminating Bias in Feedback and Promotions*, Bain & Company/Chief Executive Women.

Chamorro-Premuzic, T (2019), op. cit.

Fox, C (2017), *Stop Fixing Women: Why Building Fairer Workplaces is Everybody's Business*, NewSouth Publishing.

Chapter 6

Chemaly, S (2018), *Rage Becomes Her: The Power of Women's Anger*, Simon & Shuster UK Ltd.

Tuner, C (2012), 'Women's ideas: Do men intentionally steal them?' *Forbes*, 3 December.

Chapter 8

Babcock, L, Recalde, MP, Vesterlund, L, & Weingart, L (2017), 'Gender differences in accepting and receiving requests for tasks with low promotability', *American Economic Review*, 107(3), 714–47.

Chapter 9

King, MP (2020), *The Fix: How to Overcome the Invisible Barriers that Are Holding Women Back at Work*, Simon & Schuster UK.

Sanders, M, Zeng, J, Hellicar, M & Fagg, K (2015), *The Power of Flexibility: A Key Enabler to Boost Gender Parity and Employee Engagement*, Bain & Company/Chief Executive Women.

Wright, J (2022), 'Millennial men want 1950s housewives after they have kids', *New York Post*, 7 May.

Chapter 10

Hyman, M & Shukla, K (2019), 'A simple but profound solution to food waste', *The Doctor's Farmacy* podcast, Episode 68.

Chapter 11

Morrison, D (2013), 'Address by the Chief of Army Lieutenant General David Morrison, AO', United Nations International Women's Day Conference, 8–9 March.

Brown, B, Guillen, B (2022), 'Gathering together for the first time', *Dare to Lead* podcast, 9 May.

Chapter 13

Witherspoon, R (2015), 'Ambition is not a dirty word', 2015 *Glamour* Women of the Year Awards; transcript available at Moeslein, A (2015), 'Reese Witherspoon's moving speech at *Glamour*'s 2015 Women of the Year Awards: "Like Elle Woods, I do not like to be underestimated."', *Glamour*, 9 November.

Priestley, A (2022), 'Kristy Chong's $140 million sale of Modibodi highlights value of addressing the "unmentionable"', *Women's Agenda*.

Priestley, A (2022), 'Kindness wins as female-founded gaming studio secures record investment', *Women's Agenda*, 21 June.

Hewlett, SA (2009), 'Too much testosterone on Wall Street?', *Harvard Business Review*, 7 January.

Chapter 14

Ferguson, K, Fox, C (2018), *Women Kind: Unlocking the Power of Women Supporting Women*, Murdoch Books.

March, B (director) (2021), *Mothers of the Revolution*, General Film Corporation.

Priestley, A (2022), 'Women running outside the major parties are the story of this election', *Women's Agenda*, 21 May.

About Anneli

Anneli is on a mission to humanise the leadership landscape and change the way we see each other.

A multi-award-winning professional, Anneli's passion for decoding people and performance dynamics makes her a sought-after speaker, mentor and gender equality expert.

With her keynote speaking, mentoring and flagship programs on Women@Work, and Applied Allyship, Anneli has become the trusted advisor for many executives and organisations wanting to create inclusive cultures.

Anneli brings her gender advocacy to individuals and organisations, creating safe spaces to explore the issues and opportunities of inclusion and belonging in practical and profound ways.

To Anneli, workplace equality is not only about policies; it's also about the daily practices that support them. This is not about eradicating our human bias, but about humanising our leadership habits.

Oh and she's also a nifty parallel parker, a keen rollerblader and a salsa-dancing addict who loves any meal cooked by someone else. She lives with her husband and daughter in Melbourne, Australia.

More from Anneli

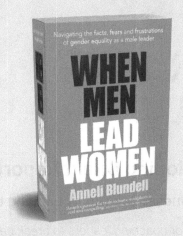

When Men Lead Women

Navigating the Facts, Fears and Frustrations of Gender Equality as a Male Leader

*A pocketbook about the unspoken responses of men
to the rise of women at work.*

Men are grappling with their place in the fight for gender equality. This short book is an attempt to surface the conversations that feel taboo – the ones that may be unpopular, and perhaps a little too controversial to say out loud.

The ideas in this book provide the pathway forward for a new dialogue between men and women: a dialogue where blame and fear are replaced with clarity and courage, and men feel not only encouraged to get involved, but crucial to the cause.

Grab your copy here: www.anneliblundell.com/books

Developing Direct Reports

Taking the Guesswork Out of Leading Leaders

*A guidebook for coaching leaders to break bad habits
and accelerate leadership performance.*

Human behaviour is complex. Developing leadership in others takes more than knowing the theory and authorising the training budget.

Written for leaders who lead leaders, this book explores the 12 most common, globally recognised leadership derailers and how to address them.

Packed with examples, insights and recommendations, and supported by a practical framework, this book is a how-to guide for leveraging the potential of your people.

Authors: Anneli Blundell, Belinda Cohen, Corrinne Armour.

Grab your copy here: www.anneliblundell.com/books